||||||||||||||||||||||||||||
D1491019

Pentecost or
The Work of God
in Philadelphia

—— A.D. 1858 ——

Calvary Chapel
PHILADELPHIA

PUBLISHER'S NOTE

It is with much joy that we bring back into print, *Pentecost or The Word of God in Philadelphia A.D. 1858*.

We have chosen to reprint the book as it was originally published in 1859. We have not updated the language nor the grammar as we wanted to stay faithful to how it was written.

We trust you will be blessed by what you read!

Calvary Chapel of Philadelphia

Pentecost or the Work of God in Philadelphia

Reprinted 2013

Calvary Chapel of Philadelphia
13500 Philmont Ave.
Philadelphia, PA 19116
www.ccphilly.org

ISBN: 978-0-9835950-3-8

Cover photo and internal artwork: © Thinkstock

Originally published in 1859 by Parry & McMillan.

FOREWORD

"It will generally be found, that when God is about to bestow any remarkable favour on a person or people, He previously pours out upon them a spirit of earnest supplication for it."

These are the opening words of the book you are holding in your hands.

At a time when we seem to have lost our way—to be in need of some compass, some guiding hand to correct our course—these words seem to me to resonate with hope, with promise from the one who does not break a bruised reed or quench a smoking flax.

They seem to beckon us anew to prayer, to seek His face, to believe that Jesus is the same yesterday, today and forever, and that He is as inclined to revive His church today as He was in Philadelphia in 1858.

Oh Lord, do it again.

Pastor Joe Focht
Philadelphia 2013

THE

YOUNG MEN'S CHRISTIAN ASSOCIATION
of PHILADELPHIA

Was established in the year 1854, with the view of uniting and directing the efforts of Christian young men, as an auxiliary to the church of Christ.

Its Fundamental Rules Are:

I. That the object of the Association be the improvement of the spiritual, mental, and social condition of young men.

II. That the means employed for the attainment of this objective: Devotional Meetings, Lectures, Lyceum, a Library for reference and circulation, Reading-Rooms, Committees to seek out young men taking up their residences in Philadelphia and procure for them suitable boarding-houses and employment, and, by introducing them to members of the Association, throw around them Christian influences, and secure their attendance at places of worship on the Sabbath.

The Rooms of the Association are in the second story of 1009 and 1011 Chestnut Street, and are open daily (Sabbaths excepted) from 8 a.m. to 10 p.m. They are handsomely fitted up, and regularly supplied with one hundred of the most important Newspapers, Magazines, and Reviews (both religious and secular) published in this country and Europe.

All young men (especially strangers) are cordially invited to visit the Rooms.

An Annual Report, with a list of Devotional Meetings, (about thirty in number), and particulars of the operations of the Association, may be had on application to the Corresponding Secretary.

Donations of funds for the Association, or books for the Library, will be received with much gratitude, by the President, George H. Stuart, 13 Bank St., or by the Corresponding Secretary, John Wanamaker, 1009 and 1011 Chestnut St.

PENTECOST

OR

THE WORK OF GOD IN PHILADELPHIA

A.D. 1858

PREPARED BY

The Young Men's Christian Association

WITH A SUPPLEMENT

"And there was great joy in that city." —ACTS 8:8

"Tell them to stand up for Jesus."
—DYING WORDS OF REV. DUDLEY A. TYNG

PHILADELPHIA:

PARRY & McMILLAN

1859

Stereotyped by L. Johnson & Co.

PHILADELPHIA

COLLINS, PRINTER

PREFACE

"THE works of the Lord are great, *sought out* of all them that have pleasure therein." (Ps. 111:2) We are commanded to "consider" them, to "talk" of them, to "declare" them to others, as well as to "rejoice" in them ourselves. When Paul and Barnabas returned to Antioch, we are told that "they gathered the Church together, and *rehearsed all that God had done with them,* and how he had opened the door of faith unto the Gentiles." The words of the "beloved Physician" are very suggestive. When doors are opened that before were closed, it is surely a matter of great rejoicing.

The object of these pages is twofold—viz., to RECOGNIZE the present WORK OF GOD in our city, and to EXTEND the knowledge of it here and elsewhere.

The Committee of fifteen (one from each evangelical denomination represented in the YOUNG MEN'S CHRISTIAN ASSOCIATION) have felt alike the difficulty, the delicacy, and the responsibility of their trust. To enter into their work with "a single eye," to collect *authentic facts,* to let these facts speak for themselves alike to both the intelligent Christian and the candid man of the world—this, and this only, has been their aim. If they have failed, they have, at least, "done what they could." If their labours have been crowned with success, to God alone be all the glory!

At a meeting of the Young Men's Christian Association, December 27, 1858, it was further ordered that the preface should contain the resolutions passed and the names of the committee appointed September 6, 1858—viz.: "*Whereas,* very great interest is manifested all through the State for definite and authentic information as to the present work of God in Philadelphia. *Whereas,* this Association, possessing as it does such peculiar facilities for collecting and verifying the various incidents and statistics, is naturally looked to as the source from which it might most appropriately emanate. Therefore,

"*Resolved,* that, in the absence of anything else of this kind, it is exceedingly desirable that a tract of four-and-twenty (afterwards enlarged) pages should be issued at as early a period as possible, containing such an account of this work of the Holy Spirit as may be best calculated to promote its extension here and elsewhere."

COMMITTEE

REV. GEORGE DUFFIELD, JR.	Presbyterian (N.S.)
JAMES S. MARTIN	Reformed Presbyterian
GEORGE S. FOX	Protestant Episcopal
JOHN C. BLISS	Independent
JOHN WIEST	German Reformed
WILLIAM GETTY	United Presbyterian
GEORGE O. EVANS	Baptist
T. ESMONDE HARPER	Presbyterian (O.S.)
JOHN M. DUTTON	Methodist Episcopal
JOHN F. GRAFF	Reformed Dutch
ELLWOOD B. DAVIS	Society of Friends
WILLIAM ROWZEE	Disciples of Christ
F. B. ATMORE	Methodist Protestant
HENRY B. ASHMEAD	Lutheran
D.M. WARNER	Moravian

Signed by order of the Association,

GEORGE H. STUART, President

John Wanamaker, Cor. Secretary

Philadelphia, Dec. 28, 1858

THE
WORK OF GOD
IN PHILADELPHIA

"It will generally be found, that when God is about to bestow any remarkable favour on a person or people, He previously pours out upon them a spirit of earnest supplication for it." So said a pastor in Philadelphia, nearly a hundred years ago. The principle is undoubtedly a correct one. GOD LEADS HIS PEOPLE TO PRAY FOR THAT WHICH HE DESIGNS TO GIVE. Thus it was previous to the great day of Pentecost, when the disciples "continued with one accord in prayer and supplication, with the women and Mary the mother of Jesus, and with his brethren." Thus it was at the commencement of the Reformation, in the sixteenth century, and of the "Great Awakening," in the last. So is it still, when a risen Saviour is once more standing in the midst of his disciples, breathing upon them, and saying, "Receive ye the Holy Ghost." (John 20:22)

This mighty work began in PRAYER, "under the fig tree," (John 1:48), and prayer is the key by means of which to unlock its entire history. The same voice of the Lord that had spoken *to* his people in his Providence, had already been speaking *in* them by the "still small voice" of the Holy Spirit. It is in evidence, the most authentic and definite, before those entrusted with the compilation of these pages, that as early as January 1856, there were not a few who were

11

led to pray, "O Lord, revive THY work," and to engage in united prayer for this purpose. "Scores of richly-laden vessels," said they, "are now lying in the river a few miles below our city, anxiously waiting to reach our wharves. Why this delay? *Because the channel is closed by the ice.* Thus it is with the exceeding great and precious promises of God. Not only is He willing, but He is *waiting* to bestow them upon us. Why does He not bestow them? Alas! Prayer is indeed the appointed channel through which the blessing flows; but *the channel is not open by which for God to communicate, or for us to receive it.* It is because we RESTRAIN prayer, that the things that remain are ready to die."

The spirit of prayer thus so graciously revived in the hearts of some of God's people for themselves, in the month of October, A.D. 1851, took a more extended range; "Open thy mouth wide, and I will fill it," (Ps. 81:10) was the message that came to many a closet. "Pray for this city, this great and wicked city," was the suggestion constantly pressing upon those who loved to pray; they must *pray for it specifically,* if they prayed at all.

Soon the stream of prayer, overflowing the hearts of individual suppliants in the closet, found its way into the various churches. Christians began to love the place where prayer was wont to be made, and to assemble there in unusual numbers. This increase of interest in the church prayer-meeting naturally suggested union prayer-meetings for the entire denomination; each church, in regular succession, being visited by those who loved to pray for the others, and all the churches for the time-being making but one church for this purpose. These "union" meetings were held at different seasons; some early in the winter, some later, and some in the following spring; and at different times, some in the afternoon, others in the evening; some once a week, others more frequently. The testimony from all the different denominations as to the delightful influence of thus coming together, as "with one accord," for prayer and supplication, was one and the same. Once more the dew was on the fleece, the "little cloud" above the horizon, and it was manifest to the feeblest faith that again the Lord had "spoken good concerning Israel."

But a higher and still more perfect and glorious development of the SPIRIT OF PRAYER was yet in reserve. Simultaneously with the outpouring of the "spirit of grace and supplication" on the different churches, by the great Head of the church, it also pleased Him to pour out upon them, in a most remarkable degree, like the precious ointment on the head of Aaron, the spirit of CHRISTIAN UNION. The impassioned appeals of Rev. Dr. Duff; an anniversary at the Musical Fund Hall, where addresses were made on this subject by various ministers, and one in particular by the Rev. Dudley A. Tyng; the "union" prayer-meetings on Thanksgiving-day; the invitations freely extended to ministers of different ecclesiastical bodies, to occupy the pulpits of other denominations; and occasionally a series of Sabbath evening discourses, delivered in the same church by representatives of all the different denominations in the city; these and many similar circumstances announced as plainly what was coming, as ever the bright purple clouds in the east announced the rising of the sun! Almost as by a simultaneous consent, it became evident to all that it was not the things in which the followers of Jesus *differed* that made them Christians, but those in which they were *agreed;* that they were not distant connections, but blood relations through Him who shed his blood in common for them all; that, whatever might be their particular state, they were all of the same nation; whatever their particular tribe, they all belonged to God's ONE ISRAEL. "That they all may be ONE, as Thou, Father, art in me, and I in Thee, that they also may be one in us; *that the world may believe that Thou hast sent me,*" —this was the spirit of their daily and most importunate supplication; and, even 'while they were yet speaking, graciously was it heard and answered. The "golden age" in the civil history of our Commonwealth was again renewed in her spiritual history, and on every hand was heard the exclamation, "Behold how these brethren love one another!"

The Spirit of God having thus so wonderfully prepared the *hearts* of his people for this work, it remained for the providence of God to supply some appropriate INSTRUMENTALITY. Accordingly, on the 23d of September, 1857 in the Fulton Street Prayer-meeting, New York, He gathered together, almost unknown to those who first composed the meeting, the simple elements of moral power which in their combination were to be so wonderfully effective. BUSINESS MEN, men of every denomination, at the hour of noon, were to meet daily for the great purpose of INTERCESSORY PRAYER; to these meetings those "out of Christ" were to be invited; exhortations given to them, prayers offered specifically *for* them, if they so desired it themselves, or if it was desired by their friends; with what result, is now known to the world!

Among those who attended the first "Business-Men's Prayer-Meeting" in New York, was a young man not yet twenty-one years of age. As good had resulted from these meetings in one city—why might not equal good be done by them in another? Surely it was worth the effort. Some of his fellow-members of the Young Men's Christian Association, with whom he conversed, being of the same opinion, and promising their cooperation in the matter, he applied to the Trustees of the Methodist Episcopal Union Church, Fourth Street below Arch, for the use of their lecture-room. The request was promptly complied with, and the first noon prayer-meeting in the city of Philadelphia was held in the Union Church, Nov. 23, A.D. 1857. Was it a mere coincidence that this precious gem was planted on the spot consecrated by the prayers and labours of the immortal WHITEFIELD?

For a time, however, the response on the part of the businessmen was far from encouraging; thirty-six being the highest number present, and the average attendance not exceeding twelve. At length it was deemed expedient to remove the meeting to a more central position; and the ante-room of the spacious Hall of Dr. Jayne having been generously granted by him for this purpose, the first meeting was held there Feb. 3, 1858. Even then the increase in numbers was very gradual, indeed: first twenty, then thirty, forty, fifty, sixty persons—so little did "the kingdom of God," in the first instance, "come with observation."

But now, almost as in an instant, the whole aspect of affairs underwent a most surprising change. "By Monday, March 8," says one, "the attendance in the smaller apartment of the Hall had reached three hundred, and by the next day, it was evident that many were going away for want of room. The brethren present, with much fear for the result, yet apparently led by Providence, on Tuesday, March 9, voted to hold the meeting the next day, at twelve o'clock, in the large Hall. It was our privilege to be present at that time—Wednesday, noon. The centre of the Hall has seats for twenty-five hundred people, and it was filled. The entire Hall *seats* more than four thousand. The next day it was filled again, *with the galleries,* and still it was obvious there was not room for the people. The curtain was therefore drawn away from before the stage, and the large platform thrown open to the audience. The next day, (Friday) the partition between the smaller and larger rooms was taken down, and the Hall from street to street thrown open.

"The sight is now grand and solemn. The Hall is immensely high. In the rear, several tiers of elegantly-ornamented boxes extended from the ceiling, in a semi-circular form, around the stage, or platform; and on the stage, and filling the seats, aisles, and galleries, three thousand souls—at once, on one weekday after another, at its busiest hour—bow before God in prayer for the revival of His work. Ministers and people, men and women, of all denominations or of none, all gather, and all are welcome.

"There is no noise; no confusion. A layman conducts the meeting. Any suitable person may pray or speak to the audience for three minutes only. If he does not bring his prayer or remarks to a close in that time, a bell is touched, and he gives way. One or two verses of the most spiritual hymns go up like the 'sound of many waters;' requests for prayer for individuals are then read; one layman or minister succeeds another in perfect order and quiet, and, after a space which seems a few minutes, so strange, so absorbing, so interesting is the scene, the leader announces that it is one o'clock, and, punctual to the moment, a minister pronounces the benediction, and the immense audience, slowly, quietly, and in perfect order, pass from the Hall; some ministers remaining to converse, in a small room off the platform, with any who may desire spiritual instruction.

"No man there—no man, perhaps, living or dead—has ever seen anything like it. On the day of Pentecost Peter preached, Luther preached, and Livingston, and Whitefield, and Wesley! Great spiritual movements have been usually identified with some eloquent voice; but NO NAME, except the name that is above every name, is identified with this meeting."

"Yes," said a clergyman on the following Sabbath, "Think of the prayer-meetings this last week in Jayne's Hall, literally and truly unprecedented and unparalleled in the history of any city or any age. Wave after wave pouring in from the closet, from the family, from the church, from the 'Union Prayer-Meetings,' until the great tidal or tenth wave rolled its mighty surge upon us, swallowing up for the time-being all separate sects, creeds, denominations, in the one great, glorious, and only Church of the Holy Ghost! God is with us, of a truth!"

But even these descriptions fall short of the real extent of religious feeling in the city at large. Jayne's Hall, immense as it was, was not the only place where Christians of every name met for the purpose of united prayer. Towards the close of that same Pentecostal week, a Union Prayer-meeting was called in a church conveniently situated in the northern part of the city. At the hour appointed, some twenty persons might have been seen slowly making their way through the unbroken snow-drifts, to keep their faith with God and with each other. But from the very moment that they crossed the threshold, it was manifest that God was with them of a truth, and that the blessing was "coming" to them also. On Friday afternoon it came in all its fullness. The large lecture-room (capable of holding some five hundred persons) was crowded to overflowing. The number of requests on the table for prayer was so great that the leader only looked at them with wonder, and did not pretend to read them. "Doubtless," said he, "we all feel just in the same way for our unconverted friends and relatives. For my own part, I must ask you to pray for my children." "For my two sons and a daughter," said a second. "For my father," said a third. "For my husband," said a lady, with a tenderness and energy that thrilled through every soul; and thus, in less than three minutes, a hundred similar requests were presented throughout the whole room. Then, as with one accord, the entire congregation lifted up their voices and wept together. The place was indeed a BOCHIM; and of all the scenes that have been witnessed during the revival, perhaps there was none more perfectly characteristic and overwhelming. A few days after, at this same meeting, the people of God, as by a common impulse, rose to their feet, and there, standing before the Lord, solemnly consecrated themselves afresh to his service. The history in detail of that single meeting would constitute a volume of itself. Out of many incidents, we select but one.

At the close of a meeting, a lady approached a little group of ministers and others, and called one of them aside to speak with him. "I could not find it in my heart," said she, "to leave this room, until I told what God had done for my soul. I came here this afternoon in darkness, heavily burdened with my sin, and well-nigh in despair; but, during the third prayer, I felt as if I could believe on Christ: peace came to my soul, and *now I must go home and tell mother!*" The tone of voice, the expression of countenance, the tears rolling down her cheeks, and joy meanwhile beaming from her eyes, it is utterly impossible for us to describe. Conversion was to her a change as *real* as for one asleep to awake; for a captive in darkness and in a dungeon to come out into light and liberty; for one who before was blind to be made to see; for one who was dead to be made alive.

The lecture-room having become too strait for the multitude of worshippers, similar Union prayer-meetings were established farther west and north, in the afternoon; and also in the Handel and Haydn Hall at noon—the attendance at the latter place amounting at times to a thousand or twelve hundred persons.

Taking all the Union prayer-meetings together, independent of the regular church-meetings in the evening, the number of those who daily met for prayer about this time was at least FIVE THOUSAND.

In connection with the Union prayer-meetings, as if by common consent, "union preaching" was also established. That all might feel equally free to attend, the favourite place for such preaching was the great public halls, such as Jayne's, Handel and Haydn, and the American Mechanics'; and, what is very significant, all of them were freely tendered by the proprietors for the use of the people, without expense. The time appointed for these services was usually on the afternoon of a weekday, or at such an hour on the Sabbath as would not interfere with public worship in the churches. Two sermons in this course, by the Rev. Dudley A. Tyng, one on the words, "COME; for all things are now ready," and the other on, "Ye that are men, serve the Lord," —will never be forgotten—especially the latter, when the congregation at Jayne's Hall numbered at least five thousand. The way of God in the sanctuary was wonderful indeed. The gospel came not in word, only, but in power.

At these meetings, also, multitudes of tracts and books, some of them original, and some whose value had been tested by their circulation for more than half a century, were freely distributed at the doors to those who were retiring from the meetings. It seemed as if every Christian brother or sister, who had been benefited by any particular tract, could not rest until they had provided a copy for others. The favourite tract was the one entitled "Come to Jesus." COME, was the great watchword of the day. And if there was one text heard more frequently than another, and one in the spirit of which Christians were most earnestly endeavoring to act, it was Rev. 22:17, "The Spirit and the bride say, COME. And let him that heareth say, COME. And let him that is athirst, COME. And WHOSOEVER will, let him take the water of life, FREELY!"

Meanwhile, the increase of attendance at public worship on the Sabbath, and the number of churches opened for services during the week, was beyond all precedent. During the latter part of the winter, rarely indeed would you pass in the evening the lecture-room of an evangelical church that was not lighted up for prayer or preaching. Sometimes even the main body of the church itself was not able to accommodate the multitude of worshippers. In some, these services had commenced months or weeks before, and were only continued; in others, they were now held for the first time; in all, there were the manifest indications of the presence and power of the Holy Spirit. The action of the Union meetings upon the churches, and of the churches upon the Union meetings, was reciprocally delightful and profitable. No rivalry—no collision. The revival spirit was alike one and the same everywhere; the same "spiritual songs;" the same fervent intercession for sinners; the same earnest invitation to come to Jesus and receive His REST; rest for the mind in His truth—for the heart in His love.

As with individuals, there were diversities of operation by the same spirit, many gladly receiving the word, and receiving it at once, others lingering in the usual way—so was it with the CHURCHES. At one time the "promise of the Father" came as the dew; at another, as the copious shower; at still another, as "the rushing of a mighty wind," all-powerful and unexpected. "On Sabbath, the 7th of March," says one of our pastors, "I entered my pulpit, weak from recent illness, and wondering whether the thickly-springing 'thorns' would continue to 'choke the word,' as usual. The day was damp and cold without; the temperature almost equally chilly and uncomfortable *within*. I did not know that there was one awakened soul in the entire congregation. Yet, before the day was over, there were thirty cases of awakening brought to light, and six of hopeful conversion. In the afternoon, especially, at a joint meeting of parents and Sabbath-school teachers to pray for the children, the Holy Spirit was poured out in such a surprising manner and to such a wonderful extent as I had never seen it before. *The spirit of prayer*, which a few days before had begun to manifest itself in two or three of the very youngest members of the church, now became almost universal. If we saw not the 'tongue of fire,' at least we *heard* it. For a series of weeks, meetings were held every evening, sustaining themselves simply by voluntary exhortations and prayers, without the necessity of a single sermon, except upon the Sabbath. Cases of conviction, and many of conversion, during prayer, left no doubt of its efficacy. The rapidity of conversion was beyond all parallel, and for the young converts to begin at once to pray and labour for the salvation of others, was recognised by them simply as a matter of course." Eight months later testimony from the same witness is equally favourable as to their continued zeal and spirituality, thus giving, by their "fruits," evidence the most conclusive and satisfactory that they were "born of God."

While such wonders as these were transpiring all through the city, public attention and interest were awakened in them in no ordinary degree. In vain was an occasional cry raised here and there of "priest-craft," "enthusiasm," "fanaticism." No definition of these terms seemed at all applicable to the case in hand. In vain did the boldest of the transgressors endeavour to rally an organized opposition; the disposition "to cease from the instruction that causeth to err," left the synagogues of Satan deserted and desolate. In vain was every subtle expedient resorted to, to involve the followers of Christ in angry and unprofitable controversy. "Speaking the truth in love," and believing that the best way to refute error was by teaching the truth *as it was in Jesus,* they humbly relied on the Holy Spirit to make the truth manifest in every man's conscience. The worse the man, the more did Christians pity him; the greater the enemy, the more did they pray for him. On one occasion, at the noon prayer-meeting, Nena Sahib himself was proposed as a subject of prayer, and by whom, of all other persons in the world, but by a Christian mother whose own son was one of the missionaries so foully murdered by him on the Ganges!

As to the impression made upon the minds of Christians generally by this new and wonderful state of things, perhaps as fair an illustration as any may be found in the remarks of a good old coloured sister, one morning when returning from a sunrise prayer-meeting in the "Canvas Church:"

"The day this great revival first broke out," said she, "that is, when I first heard of it—that very morning I was reading my New

Testament, in the seventh chapter of Revelation. A revival among the Methodists! and the Baptists! and the Episcopalians! and the Presbyterians! and all the churches! Bless the Lord, THE CHAPTER HAS COME! Sure enough, the four angels are standing on the four corners of the earth, and holding back the four winds; and the great angel having the seal of the living God has gone out a-sealing his servants in their foreheads; twelve thousand in this tribe! and twelve thousand in that! *No partiality with Him!* And soon the hundred and forty and four thousand, of all kindred and people and tongues, shall stand before the throne, and before the Lamb, clothed with white robes, and palms in their hands, and singing salvation to our God! Bless the Lord! I hope poor old Mary will be among them too."

Truly may it be said of the work that it has been "without partiality," and that God has been no respecter of persons. Like the rain and the sunshine, it has fallen on all the different fields of his heritage, with no invidious distinction or discrimination. "Parthians, and Medes, and Elamites, and the dwellers in Mesopotamia, and in Judea, and Cappadocia, and Pontus, and Asia, Phrygia, and Pamphylia, and in the parts of Libya about Cyrene, and strangers of Rome, Jews and proselytes, Cretes and Arabians," no matter what the ecclesiastical name of those who "hold the Head," (Col. 2:19) and believe that "Jesus is the Christ, the Son of God!" "Sons and daughters," "young men" and "old men," "servants" and "handmaidens," no matter what their *relative* position in the church or in the community! Greek or Jew, "circumcision or uncircumcision," Barbarian, Scythian, bond or free, no matter what their social position—all, without exception, have been made to acknowledge the *reality* of this gracious influence of the Holy Spirit; all of them, according to the number of their labourers, have gathered into their several barns their due proportion of the abounding harvest. Like the manna that lay all round about the camp, of which the children of Israel, all who were hungry, did gather, "some more, some less;" like the rock smitten at Horeb, just as much for the benefit of one tribe as another, to whose flowing waters came all who were thirsty—so has it recently been with this new and most grateful supply of the bread and water of life eternal. Literally, and without a figure, the promise of the Father has once more been fulfilled in the midst of us; and, through his only-begotten Son, in whom all fullness dwells, he has poured out of his Spirit *on all flesh!* He has blessed the house of Israel! He has blessed the house of Aaron! Blessed be his name! Of the *ten thousand* who, we hope, have been converted within the borders of our city during this YEAR OF JUBILEE, it would be utterly impossible to make a more equitable and satisfactory division among the various denominations than God by his providence and Spirit has made *already!* One denomination received 3010; a second, 1800; a third, 1735; a fourth, 1150; a fifth, 500; a sixth, 363; a seventh, 200; an eighth, 90; a ninth, 28, &c. He hath beautified the gates of Zion, alike on the East, on the North, on the South, and on the West, and the names of the twelve tribes of Israel are alike legible on them all. He who will measure with the "golden reed" of Christian charity find truth, will find that "the city lieth four square, and the length is as large as the breadth. The length and the breadth and the height of it are equal."

But to resume our narrative. It became apparent about the middle of April that the flood-tide of salvation which had thus rolled in so wonderfully upon our favoured city, was beginning to turn. The season of holy joy on the part of some of the people of God, gave place to most intense anxiety. "Has this mighty work gone deep enough into our hearts?" "In this general baptism of the Holy Spirit, are we careful to realize the necessity for an individual, personal baptism?" "Do we not need a fuller consecration to the work of Christ, one more entire and unreserved, than we have ever made before?" Such were the searching questions which God himself was soon to answer in his most solemn Providence.

Among those whose heart was with the Jayne's Hall meeting from its very commencement, and who long before had caught the blessed spirit of Christian union, like some lofty mountain the earliest rays of sunrise, was "THE CHILD OF PRAYER." Daily was he seen upon the platform, none happier than he in the belief that again the windows of heaven had been opened above us, and God was pouring out his blessing. Often did his voice of earnest exhortation, alike to saint and sinner, sound in our ears with all the clearness and sweetness of a silver trumpet. Once and again did he lead us in the great congregation, as we repeated with him, and learned again as it were, the meaning of that holy prayer which Jesus himself taught to his disciples—"OUR Father, who art in heaven: hallowed be thy name. Thy kingdom come; *thy will be done."* But ah, how soon was the sincerity of this last petition to be put to a most fearful trial!

Reminding us as he did in so many respects by his fervent and intelligent piety of that burning and shining light, John the Baptist, the great Harbinger of the Messiah, like him, also, he was cut off suddenly, unexpectedly, and in the prime of life, just at the very moment when, of all others, he was the most precious to the church of God and could the least be spared. And all that remained for us in our sore bereavement was to imitate the disciples of John, and go "and tell Jesus." That scene on the 22d of April in Concert Hall; the entire evangelical clergy of the city on the platform; the Young Men's Christian Association, of which he was an original member, in the gallery; the members of his own beloved church occupying the center of the Hall; that funeral procession along the aisle; the burst of anguish that broke forth universally throughout that immense congregation when the coffin was set down; that deeply-afflicted father; that solemn charge of Bishop McIlvaine to his brethren in the ministry, to know nothing but "Jesus Christ, and him crucified,"—will they ever be forgotten? Granted that they may be when those who were then present shall have passed away, yet that dying message, "Tell them to STAND UP FOR JESUS," will be forgotten never! Never! Never in Philadelphia! Never in America! Never in the world!

"And they embalmed him." (Gen. 1:26) Such was the text of the brother who delivered the funeral discourse; nor could he possibly have chosen one more truly or more tenderly appropriate.

It is not too much to say that with the death of the lamented Tyng came a new epoch in the history of the revival. Not in vain did the Young Men's Association adopt his message as their motto. Not in vain were the strong hands of Christian and ministerial union pledged in cordial grasp over that coffin! The mantle of his active and fraternal spirit fell upon them all. One *in* Christ! One *with* Christ! One *for* Christ! Why should it be otherwise?

Perhaps never in the entire history of the Church since the days of the Reformation were the winds and waves that too often disturb her bosom more thoroughly subdued and hushed to rest than in our city during the few days that intervened from the death of this beloved brother until his remains were committed to the tomb. Once more Christianity seemed to reach her true summit-level. The kind, fraternal and co-operative spirit that had thus been developed must, of necessity, find some appropriate sphere in which to manifest itself. It looks for a field on which to enter, and lo! white unto the harvest, it finds it in that of UNION MISSIONS.

It was asserted that, if on any given day all the evangelical churches should be filled, nearly one half of the population would be excluded for want of room. Hence the necessity, as in former times of revival, for "field-preaching" of some kind; and, after careful deliberation as to the best manner in which it could be secured, it was unanimously resolved in favour of the Union Tabernacle. The "big tent," as it is commonly called, was fitted up at the expense of some two thousand dollars, with suitable accommodation for three thousand persons, many of the contributions towards it being thank-offerings from those who had recently been converted. On Saturday, the 1st of May, it was dedicated by appropriate religious services. There was present a large concourse of people, morning, afternoon, and evening, and at least fifty clergymen, of various evangelical denominations. In the different services, representatives of no less than fifteen of these denominations took some part, and thereby gave their countenance and public approbation to the movement.

During the first two months there were fifty-three sermons preached by ministers in connection with eleven different branches of the church of Christ, and the aggregate number of those present was *fifty-one thousand*. During the four and a half months that the tent was in the city, there were held in it three hundred and thirty-three meetings—viz.: twelve inquiry-meetings, thirty-seven children's meetings, one hundred and seventeen prayer-meetings, and one hundred and seventy-nine services at which there was preaching. The number present during these various services has been estimated in the aggregate at one hundred and fifty thousand—to whom the gospel has been proclaimed by ministers in connection with nineteen different branches of the church of Christ.

The whole number of those who have professed conversion in connection with the services of the tent in the city is about two hundred. Of the multitudes of those who were convicted there, and professed their faith in various churches, we can form no estimate.

Conversion of an Old Man

One day, after a sermon on the text, "Choose ye this day whom ye will serve," an aged man made his way to the pulpit with tearful eyes, saying *he* now felt it was high time to make a decision, that the world had deceived and ruined him, and that, having a disease of the heart, he expected any moment to be called into an eternity for which he had made no preparation. "My sins," said he, "have been so many and great that I despair of any hope; and I can see myself already in the outer circle of the whirlpool of eternal death. If I had had strength, I should have stood up before the congregation, and, stretching out my skeleton hand, have bade the young look at me and take warning." Next day he came to the tent for consultation, when he remarked that "he knew historically so much of Christ, that he supposed if all the sins of all men, from the time of Adam down, could be heaped on the head of one sinner and personified in his experience, that even such a wretch Christ would be both willing and able to save, if he would but come to him; and yet, somehow," said he, "I cannot believe that there is mercy for me." He was made the subject of special and earnest prayer. The day following, he sent word from his dying bed that his doubts and fear had vanished, and all within was peace. Was not this a brand plucked from the fire?

Conversion of a Skeptic

At the closing meeting of the tent at Fourth and George Streets, a man, some thirty years of age, and of no ordinary intelligence, made the following statement, which, at the request of a number who heard him, was afterwards committed to writing:

"Passing the tent one evening, curiosity prompted me to enter. I stayed until the exercises were over, and left rather interested, determined to spend an evening or two afterwards in listening to the various views of ministers belonging to different denominations on the subject of religion. I must confess, however, that all I heard there was one great principle of the Bible—namely, *Christ's atonement for the sins of the world;* and I began to think that there must be more in religion than I had ever given it credit for, to make men spend their time and money in trying to convince others of the error of their ways. So I still continued to attend the meetings.

"The first time I really took any interest in that which concerned my soul was while hearing a sermon preached from Proverbs 9:12. It sent an arrow of conviction to my soul; and I went home persuaded that there was a God, able and willing to save, but whose stern sense of justice would compel him to punish all those who, knowing his will, defied his power. I was at that time fully aware of the fact that, for many, many years, I had walked in the highroad to destruction, heeding not the voice of conscience, keeping away from the house of God, listening to those who denied his existence, and following the pleasures of the world through all their stages, even to the verge of the drunkard's grave. Well may I love that tent! If a man never forgets the place of his earthly birth, how much more must he remember the place where he is born of God, and becomes a joint heir with Jesus Christ! I consider the thought heaven-born that caused a tent to be erected for worship in the summer season. The poor sinner will be drawn into it when you could not persuade him to enter a church. In my own case, for instance, I had heard of the great revival going on in Jayne's Hall, in the engine and hose companies, and almost in every part of the city, and yet never visited any of these places, with the exception of once going into Jayne's Hall and staying about five minutes. But, loitering about one evening, thinking of anything but religion, I entered the tent; and I, who had scarcely been in a church for the last fifteen years, became aware that there was something else than earthly pleasures—that there was a God to fear, a Saviour to love, and an inheritance in heaven for all who believe in him and follow in his footsteps."

Conversion of a Gambler

Among others who found their way to the tent one evening was a man who had long been addicted to intoxication: so completely, also, was he infatuated with the excitement of gambling, that whole days and nights were spent by him in this miserable employment. On one occasion he had gone so far as to play a game of cards on the "cooling-board" on which was lying the corpse of his own sister. But even this man was not beyond the reach of the arm that is mighty to save! He whose name is "Jesus," because *he saves his people from their sins,* has saved him from gambling, and he is now an industrious man—saved him from intemperance—and now he is a sober man, a good citizen, and a consistent Christian.

CONVERSION OF A TAVERN-KEEPER—
STRIKING INTO A NEW PATH

A man who had been brought up in a country tavern from the time he was three years of age—who had always been in the habit of using liquor, often to excess—stepped into the tent one afternoon, out of mere curiosity. Finding that they were holding a temperance-meeting for boys, he thought he would hear what they had to say. "For the first time in my life," said he, "I felt that I was a sinner, and fast hastening to a drunkard's grave. At the close of the services, hearing them offer to every boy who signed the pledge a New Testament, I determined then and there to strike into a new path. I rose from my seat, went forward to the desk, asked them to let me sign the pledge, and give me a Testament. After this, feeling that I had taken one right step, I resolved to go forward; and, returning home, I prayed to God for pardon until I found it in Jesus Christ. My father and almost our whole family are now converted. We have given up tavern-keeping, and gone to farming, happier and more prosperous in every way than when engaged in selling rum."

CONVERSION OF A GERMAN

"God has many times called me to repentance, so that I have even been led to pray for a new heart and the forgiveness of my sins. But then Satan would follow me up closely, and try to make me believe that I was good enough to go to heaven—that I was not as bad as others—that to go to church once a Sunday, and be honest and charitable, etc., was all that was necessary. This did not satisfy me, however. I felt something more was necessary than mere formality.

So I tried to serve God and mammon together—to please God in some way or other, but at the same time not give up the world. Thus both myself and my wife grew colder and colder, until suddenly God took away our only child. Feeling this to be another call to leave the world, we determined to seek Christ, that we might go to that happy place where our dear child had gone to; but we did not realize our determination. After this I entered into business, with great prospects of success; but again we saw the finger of God, and we lost almost everything we had. Thank God that we did not prosper, or we might have been lost forever. Again, therefore, we sought the Lord more earnestly than before, but, oh, we gave way again. So God took away another child, just as dear to us as the first; but another call and another determination resulted no better than the others. It was necessary that we should be afflicted still more. A third child died—then a beloved mother—then I was brought to the verge of the grave myself. But, thank God, he saved my life that he might save my soul. After going on in this miserable way year after year, at length the Tent came. Never did I feel the call of God so much, so strong, so earnestly, as there. Never before did I hear the plan of salvation laid down so simply, so distinctly, and with so much warmth and earnestness, as by the different servants of God who preached there. Each invitation seemed to be the last that we should ever receive, and we felt that it was now or never…

Thus has this blessed union tent been the means of bringing me, my dear wife and dear brother, to our blessed Redeemer!"

CONVERSION OF A TEAMSTER

Having heard that the tent was to be removed to a new locality, he went to the superintendent and asked the privilege of hauling it, *free of charge,* both now and whenever in future it was to be moved. As he "had there been born again," he wished thus to show his gratitude.

The closing services of the tent in each of the localities where it has been pitched have been solemn and affecting in the extreme. No better description can we give than this: that it was as if the good and great Physician himself had been visibly present before the multitude, and was about to take his final departure, leaving many still unhealed. The grief that is sometimes witnessed on a funeral occasion is the only comparison that will at all do justice to the overwhelming sorrow and distress of those to whom the "tent" had been their only gospel-home, and who felt as if the call was, "Come NOW to Christ, or you will never come, and be lost forever!"

Thus it was on the removal of the tent from Broad Street. Up to this time, its location had only been changed from one portion of the city to another, and was still accessible; but now that the candlestick was to be removed out of its place, men "heard as for their lives." Those who had hitherto been negligent of the invitations of the gospel were now made to feel the power of its SANCTIONS. Especially during the closing address, it seemed to us as if we were in the midst of falling thunderbolts. Nearly a hundred rose for prayer; many remained in the tent, and could scarcely be persuaded to leave it at eleven o'clock; and the inquiry-meeting the next day at a private house, so far as the distress of sinners was concerned, was Pentecost over again. For a time, praying, singing, or speaking were equally out of the question; and if ever the servants of Christ needed the tongue of the learned to speak a word in season to those that were weary, it was at that house in Fifteenth Street.

Still more remarkable was the history of the last day of the tent in Quakertown. Strictly speaking, the "Canvas Church" was not a new idea, but one that had been gradually developing itself through a series of years. The real gem of it is to be found in a "portable pulpit" used in his missionary-tour by the same brother who afterwards projected the "Union Tabernacle," and who has thus far so successfully superintended its operations. Originally the tent was designed for the country, to be used for preaching, just as the "big tent" had been employed in this State in 1855 for Temperance. Some of the heaviest contributors towards it resided in the country; and the understanding was that, after it had accomplished its mission for the time in the city, it might be removed into various counties in the State where the providence of God would indicate—particularly among the Germans.

The first place where it was pitched after leaving the city was QUAKERTOWN, a village of some five hundred inhabitants— thrifty, industrious, intelligent, but where, with the exception of a Friends' (Hicksite) meeting-house on the outskirts, there was no church, and where, until recently, such a thing as a public prayer-meeting has never been known. A field more unpromising into which to introduce evangelical truth it is very difficult to imagine. The opposition was characteristic. "The tent is a trap to make money," they said; and several days elapsed before the people could be persuaded otherwise. Even those who stood around the doors ventured in only after the strongest assurances and the most urgent and repeated invitations. But this, as it afterwards appeared, was only for the trial of our faith. The earnest, heartfelt petitions of the noon prayer-meeting in Jayne's Hall, offered daily for the success of the Union Tabernacle in its new field of operations, entered into the ear of the God of Sabaoth. Israel prevails against Amalek. The walls of Jericho fall down before the ark of the Covenant. The same gospel that, at the beginning, went forth "conquering and to conquer"—that triumphed over Judaism in Jerusalem, philosophy in Athens, sensuality in Corinth, barbarism in Melita, idolatry at Rome, and worldliness in Philadelphia—was also destined to gain no insignificant triumph in this little village of Quakertown.

After nine days of preaching, during which "the word of the Lord grew mightily and prevailed," it was determined, according to previous arrangement, to strike the tent on the 6th of October. At 2p.m. of that day, while engaged in public worship, the congregation was suddenly interrupted by a burst of youthful voices, singing the hymn:

"How pleasant thus to dwell below,
In fellowship of love!
And, though we part, 'tis bliss to know
The good shall meet above," &c.

and ending each verse with the chorus,

"Oh, that will be joyful!
To meet, to part no more,
On Canaan's happy shore;
And sing the everlasting song
With those who've gone before."

Thus singing, round and round the tent the children marched, bearing in front of them a beautiful banner, garlanded with fresh and fragrant flowers, with the motto, "WE LOVE HIM, BECAUSE HE FIRST LOVED US." As may be imagined, both the speaker and the audience were much affected by this unlooked-for testimony of the new Sunday-school children to the good that had been wrought in the tent during the time that it was pitched in their village; and, as the words "part no more," "part no more," were echoed and re-echoed through the tent, no doubt they thought of the time when Jesus made his triumphant entry into Jerusalem, and the children echoed through the temple, "Hosanna, hosanna to the Son of David!" At the close of the services, the little singers presented as a token of their gratitude four magnificent wreaths—"a perishable memorial of good imperishable." What added still further to the value of these wreaths was the fact that they were woven by the young men and young women who had been converted in the tent, and who, all the while that they were weaving them, were singing and praying for the future success of the tent in its mission of truth and love.

But it was at the close of the evening service that "the fountains of the great deep were broken up." "You saw," says an eye-witness, "the closing services of the tent in Philadelphia, and know their character; but there is no comparison between the scene in Philadelphia and at Quakertown. The latter begs all description. Would that I could paint such a picture as was given that night by the recording-angel before the throne of God! To my own mind, it appeared more like the evening after a day of battle than anything else I could think of. There were those who were rejoicing in the victory that had been achieved in the name of the Lord. There, those who, with tears of gratitude in their eyes, pressed forward to thank the Captain of Salvation for their deliverance from the captivity of Satan. There, too, in little groups, were gathered the wounded in spirit and the sorrowing in heart, with the ministers and Christians belonging to various branches of the church of our Lord standing in the midst of them and pointing to the great Physician of souls, 'by whose stripes we are healed.'

"It was eleven o'clock p.m. before the people left the tent, and then only to assemble in two different houses—the English in one and the Germans in the other—for personal conversation and prayer. There were seen, kneeling side by side in the same row, a mother, a son, and a daughter; a young married lady, her husband, her mother, two brothers, and two sisters! And, in the other house, a father, mother, four adult sons, and a daughter—constituting, with the exception of a little child, the entire family.

"The scene at the German meeting was such a one as has been very seldom witnessed. Filling the front room, the back room, the entry, the staircase, the porch, and some of them standing out of doors, were more than a hundred persons, putting the earnest inquiry, 'What must I do to be saved?'

"We continued talking and praying with them until midnight; and then, oh, how hard it was to say farewell! 'Don't leave us until we find Jesus!' exclaimed one, in the agony of her heart; and such seemed to be the feeling among them all. It was not until two o'clock in the morning that the last inquirer had left the house, and we found an opportunity to pour out our gratitude to God for the wonders he had this day wrought."

That all this was not mere temporary excitement is evident from the fact that, immediately on the tent being taken down, eleven of the prominent men of the village, representing six different denominations, organized themselves into a committee, and, on the very same lot of ground on which the tent had been pitched, erected Winter Tabernacle, eighty-five by sixty feet, which was dedicated to the worship of Almighty God, with appropriate services, November 7, 1858. They present the singular spectacle of a little community who, by the simple preaching of the gospel, are only Christians, and nothing more; and who, while they love those of every name who preach Jesus Christ and him crucified, and give them a cordial welcome, have no distinctive name of their own. The interest awakened on their behalf is intense; and we do most earnestly entreat of every Christian brother and sister into whose hands these pages may fall that they would remember in their prayers the little community of disciples at Quakertown. As yet the seamless robe has not been rent. God grant by his Spirit and his Providence that it may continue whole!

Interesting, however, as is the history of the work of God in connection with the "Tent," there is another chapter in "Union Missions" which, in some respects, at least, is still more remarkable. About the same time that services were commenced in the Tabernacle, a very deep and unusual interest began to be manifested by many Christians on behalf of the FIREMEN of Philadelphia. Numbering nearly a hundred companies, and enrolling on their lists thousands of members, active and contributing, owning for the most part their own engine and hose houses, and composed principally of young men in the very prime of life, it was easy to see why they too should be made the subjects of earnest prayer. The ties of grace, like those of nature, are not to be restricted within temporary and artificial limits. A son is a son, a brother a brother, a husband a husband, no matter what the association with which he may be identified. Hence, at a very early period in the history of the revival, sermons were delivered in churches and halls to the firemen; and in the various "Union Meetings" special prayer was made for their conversion. At length the subject was taken up by the Young Men's Christian Association; and it was resolved, after due deliberation, to commence a series of "Firemen's Prayer Meetings." "*Firemen's* prayer-meetings!" said one: "who ever *dreamed* of such a thing?"

And yet, wild and Quixotic as it seemed in the first instance, the movement has abundantly manifested itself as of the Lord.

Scarcely had the resolution been adopted, when a hose-company came forward and offered the use of their hall for a prayer-meeting, even before any application had been made to them for this purpose. The offer was promptly accepted, and the meeting commenced: at first with only a few in attendance, but afterwards, as the result of personal effort with the members of the company, with many more.

"At the first firemen's prayer-meeting," said a brother, "I saw a young man whom I was accustomed to meet daily elsewhere. It appeared my duty to speak to him about his soul. I did so next day, and found him an attentive hearer. I followed up the conversation by a letter, setting before him the finished work of Christ *for* him, and the claims of Christ *upon* him, in just such a simple form as I hoped might be blessed of the Holy Spirit. A few days after, I went to see him; but, without any apparent desire to avoid the claims of Christ upon him for his love and obedience, he seemed to think that his 'coming to Christ' must be a progressive work. I preached to him a present Jesus, able to save, willing to save, and to save him *now!* At the close of the conversation, in answer to a proposal to meet me at the throne of grace that night at ten o'clock, he at his house and I at mine, he replied, 'I never prayed in my life: I know not how to pray.' Showing him from the parable of the Pharisee and Publican what prayer was, he promised, with a full heart, to comply with my request. At noon, I went to one of our smaller union meetings and presented his case there. In the evening, I did the same thing at our own church prayer-meeting, and suggested to all who would feel it a privilege so to do to unite at the hour of ten o'clock in one supplication for that young man. The hour, I have reason to believe, was well observed. The next morning, about ten o'clock, I saw him approaching me in the street. Grasping me cordially by the hand, the tears pouring down his cheeks, and his voice almost choked by emotion, he exclaimed, 'God blessed my soul last night, while I waited before him!' …Several months have now elapsed, and he is still an humble and consistent follower of Jesus Christ."

Encouraged by the success of the first prayer-meeting, a second was soon opened in another company; and here, too, the blessing of God was almost immediately apparent—so much so that, on the 24th of March, one of its members presented himself in Jayne's Hall, and bore the following testimony to what God had done for his soul:

"I am a poor fireman. I never spoke before on any occasion; and I want you to pray for me now, that I may do what I promised God I would do almost the very moment I found peace to my soul. I attended the first prayer-meeting held in our hose-house, and there my feelings were deeply aroused. I felt I was a sinner. I knew I had no interest in my Saviour. But I felt that I wanted an interest in him; and before I left that room I resolved, with the help of God, from that night that I would forsake all my evil ways and try to serve God all the remainder of my life. Just before I made this resolve, many things came into my mind. I had one particular associate—one in whose company I always felt happy. We always went together, and I loved him. Thoughts of this kind came up: *Could I quit his company?* I knew I would have to as an associate. I knew I would have to give up all my old companions as associates, and I thank God that I felt that I could not leave that room that night without making the resolve to do so.

"As I sat and heard the different brothers exhort and offer prayer, I felt that I would like to become a Christian too. I thought that they must be really happy, and from that night I commenced to pray God to make me a Christian. I was out of employment at that time, and through the day I would go up in my room and shut myself in. I would then take the Bible and read two or three chapters, and afterwards kneel down and pray. I went on so for about two weeks, at least seven or eight times a day, but still I could not find the Saviour. I commenced getting discouraged. I had heard that the Holy Spirit would not always strive with man, and I began to feel alarmed. I would sit in my room and try to make solemn thoughts. I thought if I could get solemn then I could get on my knees and pray to God. I would try to think on God and then on hell; but I could not get the feeling I wanted. I felt as if I wanted some instruction. I could not pray aright. I determined therefore at one of the meetings in our hose-house to ask one of our brothers what I must do to become a Christian. After the meeting was over, I followed a brother to the corner. I then stopped him and told him I would like to become a Christian. I told him I had endeavoured to pray, but I could not pray feelingly. He invited me to come to the church where he attended. I did so, and was there introduced to one of the members, who asked me to call and see him the next day. I was very glad of the opportunity, but I could not get off from my business, as we were then much hurried. During the week I felt very uneasy, so much so that I could not wait any longer: so I quit my work, and went to see the brother who had invited me. When I went to see him, I was very anxious, but when I left his place, I must confess that it was with joy. The way to be saved appeared so clear and simple that I could not restrain my rapture. He clearly showed me that I could not come to God with any merits of my own; that none of my works were of any avail; that I was not to try to make myself righteous, but that I should go to Christ 'just as I am,' with all my sins, with all my unfeelingness, looking away from myself, and asking God to have mercy upon me only for the sake of Jesus Christ! That night I went home with joy, and when I went to my prayers I did go different from any time in my life. I prayed without waiting to get feeling. After I had done praying, and got up off my knees, I did not feel that God had blessed me. But some ten or fifteen minutes after I had got in bed, there was one of the happiest feelings I ever had in my life. I was so really happy that I was going to wake my bed-fellow, to tell him how happy I was. But I thought he would not know what I meant. I must have gone to sleep in this happiness, for in the morning my heart was full, and I could not rest until I told all my people and all my associates what God had done for my soul. Oh, pray for me and for all the firemen, for greatly do we need your prayers."

We are happy to add that this testimony was not given in vain, but that his "bed-fellow," and more than one of his associates, were soon found walking with him in the ways of righteousness, as once they had walked in the ways of sin.

Here is the testimony of one of them given one Saturday evening at a young men's prayer-meeting:

"I feel as though I wanted to say something to this meeting, and yet I don't know hardly what to say. My heart is full.

"I was thinking to-night, on coming to this meeting, on passing a house where I used to pass my Saturday nights, why I didn't care to spend them there anymore. I know I don't, and that I feel a great deal better to be here.

"A little thing happened to me the other night down at the hose-house. I was thinking whether I could be as good a fireman since my conversion as before, and I find I can be *a better one.* I bunk at the hose-house, and of late I have been sleeping in the meeting-room; for (and here his voice faltered) I feel that in that room I was *born again, and I love that room.* Well, we are having some repairs done to our house, and the other night the company had to turn into the meeting-room to sleep too, as the bunk-room was upside down. When my bedtime came, there were quite a number of the company in the room. Now, I am in the habit of reading a chapter in my Testament, and of offering up a prayer to God, before I go to bed. I felt that I couldn't go to sleep until I had done that; but somehow I felt a little backward there, for I was afraid that they would laugh and jeer at me. Still, I thought that it had got to be done. So I went up to the desk, turned the gas on a little brighter, opened my Testament, and began to read. It was in Matthew, a very interesting chapter, all about Judas Iscariot betraying his Master, and how sorry he was for it afterwards. This made me determine not to betray him. But, while I was reading, every man of the company kept as quiet and orderly as could be.

"After I had got through reading, I went to my settee, and surely, I thought, they would have something to say when they saw me on my knees in prayer. But I got down first on one knee and then on another, and—would you believe it? —there wasn't a noise or a remark made. Whilst I was so engaged, you might have heard a pin drop all through the room, and when I was through, I lay down and went to sleep, with a smile on my lips; and it was the happiest night in all my life.

"Now, I want to say to any young man in this room, to-night, if there is anyone here who is afraid to come out and STAND UP FOR JESUS, for fear of your companions laughing at you or making fun of you, it is a foolish feeling. I tell you, if there is any laughing, or jeering, or scoffing going on, you will not find it among firemen; and I tell you, too, that they respect me to-day more than they ever did when I was not a Christian."

On the 25th of April, one of the oldest and most influential companies in the city threw open their hall for a *daily* prayer-meeting. The hall, being unusually large, well-furnished, and in a central location, became at once a rallying-point not only for firemen, but for their mothers and sisters, for strangers, and for

Christians generally. Perhaps, next to Jayne's Hall and the "Union Tabernacle," the history of the "Diligent" meeting constitutes one of the most remarkable features in the whole revival. To see a few praying young men enter the hall of a company in which, up to that time, of its active members there was not a single member of the church of Christ; to see these young men conciliated, interested, and prevailed upon to attend the meetings; to see one after another, under the striving of the Holy Spirit, rise in their places, and thus express their desires that the people of God should remember them in prayer; to see day after day those of them who had resolved "to cease to do evil" and "learn to do well" coming out on the Lord's side, and professing their determination to "Stand up for Jesus;" eventually to see this very prayer-meeting conducted by the members of the company and sustained by their prayers and exhortations—was a sight which, considering all the circumstances of the case, the age of these young men, their previous history, and their peculiar temptations, has never known a parallel in our city.

Instead of general description, however, we submit a few extracts from the reports of the committee having the meeting in charge:

"August 28—The meetings during the past week have been characterized by a manifest presence of the Holy Spirit. Never have we witnessed such deep solemnity. The hall has been filled every afternoon, and on some occasions several were standing in the passage. On last Sabbath evening at an early hour the room was full to overflowing. Many went away unable to get seats. So large was the attendance, it was thought best to start another meeting in one of the upper stories. This second meeting numbered over a hundred, and the voice of praise and prayer and exhortation ascended and mingled together in these two rooms.

"Requests of a most touching nature are daily offered and made the subject of united prayer. One of these deserves notice. A young man who acknowledged himself in the request as being present, stated therein that he had no hope in Jesus, but he desired the prayers of the meeting in behalf of a dear sister, who was also without hope in the Saviour, and fast sinking into the grave with consumption. His desire was that the sister might go to heaven to meet Christian parents there. A most singular instance of the striving of the Holy Spirit in the hearts of poor sinners; but, we may add, by no means a *solitary* instance. The confidence of the impenitent in the power of prayer has not infrequently been such as to shame Christians themselves.

"September 4—The present week has been one of remarkable blessing. On Sabbath evening, long before the hour arrived, the principal hall in the second story was filled. The room in the third story was also filled. The room above, in the fourth story, had every seat occupied, the passage and stairway were crowded with anxious listeners, and many went away not being able to obtain seats. In the second story there was present a delegation of about twenty-five members from one company, and of twenty members from another. Unusual solemnity and earnestness characterized all the meetings, and it was a night long to be remembered.

"Some weeks ago; so great was the interest, it was thought advisable to request members of the company to remain after the dismissal of the meeting, to spend a short season in prayer. This little meeting, held at the close of the regular meeting, has been wonderfully blessed. We do not know what name to give it. There is no formality in it. A brother starts a hymn; another follows in prayer, and another, and still another. It seems like the gathering of the disciples after the death and ascension of our blessed Master. His Spirit is evidently with us, and our earnest prayer is that he may breathe upon us more and more every day. Truly, God is doing great things for his people!"

One of these supplemental meetings was a very remarkable one; but we do not feel at liberty on this account, merely because it *was* remarkable, to withhold the testimony of brethren in relation to it. Not aiming to work out any theory by what we state, we desire to be as far from suppression on the one hand as from exaggeration on the other.

"When we came out of the meeting in the second story," says a good brother, "finding that they were still singing in the fourth story, I, with several others, went up there, to join them in their worship. After prayer, and singing, the power of the blessed Spirit's influence was so felt in that room, and there was such a heavenly atmosphere pervading it, that every heart was filled with joy unspeakable. The 'baptism' came down indeed. Such a season of 'refreshing from the presence of the Lord' I scarcely ever felt before. It was worth a lifetime of trial to be permitted to enjoy it."

The tender, devotional spirit of these meetings has reminded almost all who entered them, of the "upper room" at Jerusalem. Rarely indeed has any meeting passed without the manifested presence of the Holy Spirit—that sweet melting of heart which Christians so well know, but which they find it so impossible to describe. Perhaps no better representation of the spirit of these meetings was ever given than in the remark of a lady that "it seemed to her just like family worship!" Certainly the facts in the case warrant a full development of the idea. The people of God accustomed to assemble there have felt just like one large family, and the very last question asked in reference to any of them is: To what denomination does he belong? It is the family name, the surname, that has been the dearest to them, and not the name that goes before it. Most emphatically have they all been ONE IN CHRIST JESUS.

Some of the scenes that have been there witnessed have been thrilling in the extreme. About the first week in June, when the presence of the Holy Spirit in the minds and hearts of the impenitent was a fact that admitted and received no contradiction, a prominent member of the company rose to thank God that he had found peace in believing, and was then able to "Stand up for Jesus" and confess him before men. Then, turning immediately from the chairman to the audience, his eye searching every part of the room as if to find someone in particular, he exclaimed, with an earnestness and tenderness of manner that melted every heart, "And I have a very dear friend in this room, a member of this company; I don't see him here, but I am sure he is here: he needs Christ as much as I do; I want him, I invite him, to come to Christ and find pardon for his sins also! Oh that *all* would come!" If the invitation was not accepted, it certainly was not the fault of him by whom it was extended.

Among the various collateral incidents connected with this circumstance, perhaps one that occurred at another engine-house, the Tuesday evening following, may be deemed worthy of special notice. The room was large, the meeting crowded, and the firemen in attendance principally down by the door and standing in the entry. One of the speakers, who declared that the firemen for the last few days had been the first thought in the morning and the last thought at night, and who believed that this was emphatically the firemen's accepted time and the day of their salvation, told the company that, by the grace of God, he meant to speak to them as plainly and affectionately as the converted fireman who had the last week appealed to his impenitent companion. "I wish," said he, "to walk down this aisle to-night, as Paul did through the streets of Corinth, proclaiming on the right hand and on the left, that 'Christ died for our sins.' Could I cause all your sins to pass before you in long array, or place you in the midst of the falling thunderbolts of Sinai, or suspend you by a single thread over the lake of fire, this would not suffice to bring you to repentance; you must find it at the foot of the cross; you must look on Him who died thereon; you dare not, cannot, look long at the crucified One and remain unmoved. You cannot candidly contemplate the thought that you have never thanked Jesus Christ for what he has done to save your soul, and deliberately remain his enemy by further impenitence and unbelief."

The bow was drawn at a venture, but the arrow sped home to the heart for which God intended it. At the close of the meeting, a young man, with his face buried in his hands, and sobbing audibly, presented himself as a subject of prayer. So deeply did the thought of his ingratitude pierce through and through his heart, that for some time after the meeting was over, he had scarcely physical strength to rise from his seat and leave the room. That night he found his way as an inquirer to the house of his pastor; and the next day at the noon prayer-meeting, all fear of man thrown aside, too full of joy to restrain its manifestation, his grateful exclamation was, "Come, all ye that fear God, and I will declare what he hath done for my soul!"

This confession again, in its turn, was the means of bringing out another. His heart was too full more than simply to arise in his place and thank God "that he had heard his prayers." We asked and subsequently obtained from him the following communication:

"On sitting down to write out my religious experience, I feel a prayerful anxiety that I may relate only such things as may be for edification, and that I may be kept from glorying in aught save the cross of Christ. When, however, I think that possibly one reader of these lines may be encouraged to pray without ceasing, and place all their hope upon that Saviour who has rescued me from the horrible pit, all distaste at the idea of making public the sacred communings of the Holy Spirit with my own soul vanishes.

"In my boyhood, and as a young man, I was graciously restrained from open immorality, but I was conscious in my own heart of being utterly vile in the sight of God, and often sought his face with earnest prayer. About two years ago I took part in a Sunday-school; and here let me bear my testimony to the blessed effect of this kind of work on those engaging in it, and encourage every young person to enter such a field of labour in a prayerful spirit.

"One Saturday night, after preparing my Sunday lesson, I knelt in prayer, and, ah! How well I remember that sweet opportunity! My whole soul seemed poured out before Jesus, that he would wash away my sins and plead my cause with God. It seemed to me I never had prayed so earnestly before, nor ever felt so anxious to be saved. I drew near unto God, and he seemed to draw near unto me. I felt a sweet peace come over my soul while praying, and then a joy unspeakable and full of glory was shed abroad in my heart, and I knew that my Redeemer had borne the penalty of my sins on the accursed tree. I rose from my knees and awakened my dear wife, for I could not but want to have her rejoice with me that this soul that was dead in trespasses and sins had come to life."

Affecting Appeal

At a prayer-meeting in an engine-company, a brother rose and made the following statement. "At the fire which recently occurred on Market Street, a person was entirely buried beneath the ruins, with the exception of his right arm. Attracted by his cries for relief, a fireman descended from the adjoining building and extricated him. Borne off upon a settee insensible, he did not learn the name of his deliverer. On subsequently inquiring, he heard that the friendly fireman belonged to this very company where the meeting is to-night. The man who was then saved now stands before you. *I am that man,* and I stand here to thank my deliverer; and, as the best way of which I can think to show my gratitude to him, I now invite him to JESUS, the great deliverer of the soul." The subsequent interview between the two men was deeply affecting. The invitation was received in good part by him to whom it was extended, and he promised that his soul should no longer remain uncared for.

SINGULAR CONVERSION

On one of the hottest evenings in July we attended a little prayer-meeting in a hose-company, which was of great interest to us. At least one-half of those who were present and who prayed and exhorted were converted firemen. The experience of the leader on taking the chair, briefly and unpretendingly as it was told, made upon us a very deep impression. "No man," said he, "can be more surprised than I to find myself in such a position. You all know me very well, who I am, and what I have been. (His business was to supply the company with cigars and Sunday newspapers.) One Sunday, I was sitting in my shop reading a story in a Sunday newspaper. It was called 'Truth and Honesty,' and was about a little boy. After reading it, I felt that there *was such a thing as truth,* and that, it was *better to do right than to do wrong.* These were the feelings that first brought me to the prayer-meetings; and now I hope I know what it is to believe the truth that saves the soul." We called with him afterwards at his house to see that paper. We found that he had at once abandoned his business; and now, as we write, the very paper lies before us, with the same mark it had upon it when he drew it from the desk. Many times since have we seen that strong and earnest face in prayer-meeting, but never without thinking how much more God is able and willing to do for the conversion of sinners than his people are to ask him to do it. If one man can be reached at a time so unexpected and by an instrumentality so apparently insignificant and insufficient, why not thousands and tens of thousands more?

Plain Questions and Honest Answers

Disappointed one evening in not finding any members of the company present in their hall, one of our number, leaving the prayer-meeting, went down into the room below, where most of the members were assembled, smoking and talking as usual. "I am very curious," said he, "to know just what you firemen think on the subject of religion. You have just as much right to your opinion as I have to mine—in this respect, at least, that each one of us must give an account *for himself* unto God." Perceiving that they were not unwilling he should proceed, but rather invited further inquiry, "What, for example," said he, "do you think of the BIBLE?" "Well," said one, "I believe it. G., don't you?" G. assenting, the same seemed to be the case with all, until at length one remarked, "I guess, sir, we all believe the Bible, and that them that don't believe the Bible don't come this way!" "Another question, then:

how many of you *read* the Bible?" "Ah! That is another question," said the first spokesman. "Pardon me, however, if I put it: when did you read the Bible last?" "Not since I was home." "And you?" "Not since I was at Sunday-school," "And you?" No answer. "Never read it at home or at Sunday-school?" "I never went to Sunday-school." And thus the conversation continued, until many similar questions had been asked and answered. Oh, to what multitudes of men in this city—firemen as well as others—is the holy book of God like a letter still unopened, the seal still unbroken—a letter still unread, though it comes to us bearing the image and the superscription of the King of kings himself! How large a portion of the ungodliness which we set down to the account of infidelity may with much greater propriety be attributed to *thoughtlessness!*

Swearing

"Surely there is hope for anybody if such a one as I can be received. Why, sir, for fifteen years I have been a fireman; and I used to be awfully profane—so much so that I would scarcely utter five words without an oath. And at the factory where I work I used to use such awfully blasphemous language that the men before now have actually left me and gone away to get out of the sound of my voice. If such a swearer as I has been saved, there is hope for any!"

How to Stop Swearing

Said another fireman, "God hears prayer. I *know* he does. I can prove it by my own experience. I was a dreadful swearer; and, though ashamed of it, and oftentimes resolved to give it up, no sooner was my resolution made than I would go away and swear worse than ever. But one day, after I began to feel how wicked it was to take the name of God in vain, I looked to *Jesus Christ* to help me. And he has helped me. From that day on I have not sworn an oath, nor do I feel any *desire* to swear; but it is not myself, it is all of Christ, that I have been able to achieve the victory!"

"No Swearing, Boys!"

One of the fire-companies, shortly after the revival commenced, made very earnest efforts to stem the tide of profanity which had formerly been but too prevalent among them. On one occasion, when there was an alarm of fire, the director, taking the lead as usual, suddenly wheeled round at a sound he heard, and roared through the trumpet, with a voice of thunder, "No swearing in this company, boys!" Strangely did those words sound through the darkness of the night, and there are some who will never forget them. We trust the same words will yet sound through many trumpets more.

A Sad Purpose Prevented

"Well may I thank God for that firemen's prayer-meeting, and acknowledge it, too, to his glory and my own shame! For many years I had been an orphan. I had just lost my wife. Having nothing to live for, the sooner I got out of the world, it appeared to me, the better. I had even gone so far as to meditate the time and place of self-destruction. But, passing by an engine-house, I heard singing. I went up, and found a prayer-meeting. A friend took me by the hand and invited me to Christ. Hope sprang up in my heart. I thought I would try whether there was anything in this religion;

and now I am not ashamed to say to my brother firemen that there is. It can give peace where nothing else can give it, and make you happy as you could never have believed it possible to be. 'Oh, taste, and see that the Lord is good!' "

CONVERSION BY A SINGLE WORD

"That night I felt as if I *must* go to the Firemen's Prayer-Meeting, and as if there would be a message for me. Weeks and months together had passed away, and each week and month had only added to the darkness. I began to feel as if the gate of life would never be opened to me. But, at the close of an earnest exhortation, the brother inquired, 'Will you come to Jesus NOW?' And my heart said, 'YES!' From that moment my bonds were loosed, and I have been permitted to rejoice in that liberty wherewith Jesus makes his people free."

THE FIREMAN'S DAUGHTER

At an alarm of fire recently in one of our common schools, a little girl was seen sitting very quietly, while others were rushing downstairs, greatly to their injury. "How came you not to do as the others?" asked her teacher. "Why," said the little girl, "you see my father is a fireman; and he told me if ever there was an alarm of fire in the school-house to sit perfectly still, and I would certainly be saved. I believed father, that I would be saved *by doing just what he said.*" Had every fireman the same faith in what God says about Christ that that fireman's daughter had in the word of her father, how soon would our prayers be turned to praises!

A Better Wish

In the hall of one of the companies stands an ancient speaking-trumpet under a glass case. "Would," said, a speaker on one occasion, "that, instead of my feeble voice, I could take down this trumpet and proclaim the gospel to you, so that you might be made to hear! But no! I recall that wish. It would be of no avail thus to speak to you. Only *the still, small voice* of the Holy Spirit can so speak to you as to make you hear." Only this, indeed, only the Holy Spirit, can speak the gospel to the heart.

Firemen's Consciences not the Hardest

Two influential members of a certain company opened a tavern not long since in the neighbourhood of the hose-house. Before the month was out, however, one of them gave it up. "Twenty-nine days," said he, "in the liquor-business is too much for *my* conscience!" What sort of consciences must they have who continue in it for years?

Answer to Prayer

An old sailor thus spoke one day in Jayne's Hall. "I think I know how to prize the religion of Jesus. Once on a wreck for two weeks, and the only one there who had a hope in Christ, who can tell how precious that hope was to me? Under God, I owe my religion to my mother. Fifty-three years ago, when I was only eight years old, that dear mother, but a short time before her death, clasped me in her arms, and, having prayed that we might meet in heaven, she slept in Jesus. To all human appearance, it seemed for a long time as if those prayers would not be answered.

For forty-three years I was a drunkard and a blasphemer. But I rise in this meeting to-day to testify to the efficacy of prayer, and that I have found a Saviour."

SILENT PRAYER

At one of the first prayer-meetings in Jayne's Hall, a merchant from the South, noted for his profanity and infidel sentiments, finding that the young salesman was going there to the meeting, determined to accompany him. Turning to the other customers, he said that he wished it to be distinctly understood that he went merely out of curiosity, to report what he saw when he returned home. For a while the scene seemed to make little or no impression upon him; but, towards the close of the services, Rev. Dudley A. Tyng proposed to engage for five minutes in silent prayer. For a time the great congregation was as still as the chamber of death, and afterwards the merchant was observed to be weeping. "Let us go," said he to the young man. "No," he replied: "the services will soon be over." When they left the hall, both walked some distance in perfect silence, which was at length broken by the merchant. "I never before felt," said he, "as I did to-day in that prayer-meeting. I do not know what came over me at the moment of silent prayer. I was, against my will, convinced that these people were worshipping God sincerely, and that their religion was true. I have been a scoffer at religion, a member of an infidel club, have bought and sold infidel books. But henceforth, by the help of that God whom I have hitherto rejected and defied, I am resolved to seek that religion with all my heart." Subsequent information has been received as to his union with the church, and also of the conversion of a brother in consequence of his own.

THE MINISTER'S SON

The prayers of the Jayne's Hall meeting were on one occasion requested by a minister for his son. The request was complied with, and very earnest and importunate supplication made on his behalf. A few days after, the father wrote that on his return home, he found his son very deeply convicted and earnestly inquiring what he must do to be saved. These convictions terminating in his hopeful conversion, the father and son came down together to the city; and there, in the hall to which they were attached by such sacred associations, a number of brethren, who well remembered the circumstances, had the pleasure of rejoicing with them in their joy.

THE WIDOW'S SON

Coming out from the hall one day, a lady said to us, "You know C.? Some weeks ago, his brother, away off in a distant part of the country, wrote me, proposing that, as this was a time when God was so marvelously hearing prayer, *we two should agree* to pray for C. The proposal was at once accepted and the letter mailed; but long ere it could have reached its destination, the prayer received its answer."

"GO, AND SIN NO MORE."

Meeting a poor woman one morning, we asked her to attend the meeting. At first she excused herself by saying she had work to do, but afterwards she came in and heard a prayer. That prayer touched her heart, and she found no peace until she found it at the foot of the cross. Her life, she said, had been profane; nor had she read the Bible since her childhood. She is now an humble follower of the Saviour so long neglected by her, connected with the church of Christ, and labouring to do good to others.

PRAYER, POWER WITH GOD AND MAN

A missionary, illustrating one afternoon at the "Diligent" meeting the nature and power of intercessory prayer, told the following incident, which may also stand for not a few similar ones recently witnessed in Philadelphia. "During a period of religious interest among the Choctaw Indians, to the surprise of many, a giant Indian came into one of their meetings and took his seat on a log, apparently out of mere curiosity to see what was going on. From the platform where the missionary was sitting, he saw that the entrance of the giant had been noticed by a young convert. First the convert would look at the Indian until his eyes were filled with tears, and then he would clasp his hands together and look up to heaven, as if in a perfect agony of prayer. Towards the close of the services the giant was smitten by the truth, like Goliath by the pebble. On the invitation given by the missionary for inquirers to meet him near the platform, he came forward trembling and literally tottering with anxiety and distress, asking whether there was any hope for him. Christ was freely offered to him and promptly accepted by him; and thus once more did God declare himself the HEARER OF PRAYER."

An Importunate Suppliant

"Forty years," said a mother in Israel, "was I praying for my husband, thirty years for my daughter; and God heard me for them. And ever since the people of God, at my request, prayed for my son, I feel as if God would also hear me for him." Is not this one of the secrets of the Lord that few consider and understand as they ought?

Sad Cases

We read in the Gospels of a poor woman who "had suffered many things of many physicians, and spent all that she had, and was nothing bettered, but rather grew worse;" fit emblem and but too faithful a representative, this suffering *body,* of many a still more deeply afflicted and suffering *soul!* The number of persons of this description who have been brought to light and who have known the healing touch of Christ's garment during this present revival has been quite large. It is not the least of the recent wonders of God among us that prayers should be awakened and heard for them also. Take a single example. A lady who had been for many years a member of the church, but who had long been convinced that she had never experienced a change of heart, was led by the Holy Spirit to feel how vain a thing it was to have the "form of godliness" without the "power." She had read, "Whoso covereth his sins shall not prosper, but whoso confesseth and forsaketh them shall have mercy." Accordingly, she acted on this advice, and at length opened up her mind fully to a Christian friend. It pleased God at once to enlist his Christian sympathy on her behalf. He prayed with her, he prayed for her; he promised, on one single condition, that he would stand by her in her spiritual trouble, no matter whether it was months or years, until he saw her through it. The condition was this: that she should not deprive him of the power to help her by *leaning* upon his prayers. The solemn agreement was made; but darker and darker did the shadows gather around her soul, until the eclipse became total. What was to be done? "Ask still more prayer," said her friend. That very night an opportunity was afforded at the close of a prayer-meeting; and, heavy as the cross was, she resolutely took it up, and "rose for prayer." That prayer, we trust, was not in vain; and, ere the week was over, such a peculiar combination of the word and the providence and the Spirit of God occurred that the hard heart was broken and the stubborn will subdued. We scarcely know whether the encouragement to prayer appeared the greatest to the lady herself, to her friend, or to the members of the prayer-meeting where the special petition had been offered on her behalf.

The sympathy of Christians in endeavouring to bring sinners to Christ has been tender and affectionate in no ordinary degree. On one occasion, at Jayne's Hall, when those who desired the prayers of God's people were requested to signify it by rising or by holding up their right hand, an incident occurred, the spirit of which for the moment reminded us of the time when Jesus of Nazareth passed by in the days of his flesh, and when, "seeing *their* faith," (i.e. the faith of the friends of the sufferer,) he spake the word, and the cure was instant and complete! Twice, but in vain, a lady had endeavoured to lift up her hand. The third time, the friend beside her assisted her to raise it up, both of them being completely overpowered by their emotion. Perhaps there were not more than two or three who witnessed the occurrence; but by one, at least who did see it, it was a sight never to be forgotten.

CONVERSIONS FROM ERROR

OF A UNIVERSALIST

"Such I was," said one, "by belief; that is, I tried to make myself believe in the doctrine of universal salvation, and thought I did believe it. But, after all, I did not candidly believe it in my heart. When I thought of the death of friends it would make me shudder. One Sunday, I said to my wife, who belonged to the Society of Friends, 'Suppose we go to church to-day?'

" 'Well,' said she, 'if your conscience so dictates, let us do it.' First we went to a church in B. Street; and, after we had entered, I happened to remember that it had no steeple! More out of ridicule than anything else, I said to my wife, 'Let us go to a church with a steeple on it.' Notwithstanding her reproof, I would and did go to the steeple-church. Never was I so affected by a sermon in my life. I went home uneasy and troubled, and continued so for days, but without letting anyone know it. The first time the minister called, I told him 'it was all humbug.' Some days after he called again, and, among other remarks, made the following:—"Had you not a mother, and did she not teach you a prayer?' The appeal was more than I could stand, and that single remark had more force in it than if he had talked to me all day. 'Now,' said he, 'try and think what that prayer was that your mother taught you.' And, with these words, he bade me 'good-morning.' Weeks and months passed on, but I could find no peace nor rest until I found it in believing in Jesus."

CONVERSION OF A UNITARIAN

"Among the many cases of conversion," writes a friend, "in this special outpouring of the Holy Spirit, is one of unusual interest, not only from the important social position held, but in the radical change wrought in the whole life and character. A lady of cultivated intellect, a bold thinker, impressing her opinions on all with whom she came in contact, became involved with the ensnaring fallacy of Unitarianism. In settling down in this belief she was aided by one of her own sex, equally educated and accomplished, who confirmed her in this fatal error. By mutual conference each strengthened the other, until at length the resolution was taken to join the Unitarian Church.

"In this state of mind the claims of the gospel were presented to her, but only to be most strenuously resisted. Salvation by a crucified Redeemer was indeed to her 'a stone of stumbling and a rock of offence.' To a friend of hers who was privileged to labour with her, she replied, with an emphasis characteristic of the carnal mind, which is 'enmity against God,' 'If I accept Jesus Christ on the terms which you propose, YOU MAKE ME A DEBTOR TO HIM!' Amid much discouragement, yet with a constant presentation of the 'truth as it is in Jesus,' the Holy Spirit, after many months of unbelieving rejection, was pleased to discover 'Christ crucified,' as the only way to God. Then came the struggle to submit to the 'righteousness which is by faith in Christ.' Weeks passed by in the vain hope of satisfying God by a righteousness of her own. But the textbook used during this season of trial was the word of God. 'Thus saith the Lord,' was the answer to all the cavils of unbelief and all the reasonings of philosophy falsely so called. At length, when human reason failed to unravel the great truths of revelation, it was suggested by her friend, as the conclusion of the whole matter, 'Shall not the Judge of all the earth do right?' and there he rested the subject. It pleased God to make that declaration of his own word the means of settling her perplexed and bewildered mind. She rested on it, and found peace in believing on Jesus. Shortly after, she wrote to her Unitarian friend; and an extract from that letter will give you, perhaps, a better idea of the work of the Holy Spirit on her heart than mere general description:

" 'For several days I have had a letter on hand to send you, and have written and re-written it from the difficulty I found in saying just what I wanted. Now, however, I feel that the simplest way is the best, and that I ought no longer to delay in confessing my Saviour before men. Indeed, I long to confess him, though it be in weakness and with much trembling. Let me confess him to *you*, my dear friend, and let me ask you to listen patiently to what are now the dearest and deepest thoughts of my life. And yet, what can I say? JESUS DIED FOR ME! One thing only I know:—"Whereas once I was blind, now I see." I see him, my Redeemer, my Sanctifier, my ever-present Lord and Master! Above all, I see him an all-sufficient atonement for my sins; and at the sight the weary burden has fallen from me, and left me free in that liberty wherewith Christ has made me free. Oh, if I could but find words to express to you the deep inward peace and joy which has been mine at intervals for the last few weeks, Dear --, I think it would touch your heart! I have honestly, I think, been praying and seeking to be enlightened with the true light from above; and gradually, almost insensibly, I have been drawn nearer and nearer unto Jesus of Nazareth, until at last, weary, sin-sick, and unworthy, as I know I am, I have fallen at the foot of the cross, and have sought and found mercy. It is unspeakably precious to me to have been thus bought; and oh, I would not exchange this all-sufficient Saviour, and the salvation which is his free gift, (and oh, *how* free!) for all the righteousness which years or centuries of perfect obedience to the law might win for me! I *glory* in the cross of Christ!

" 'Yet I write these words in fear and trembling, lest through my unfaithfulness I may bring reproach on the cause I long to serve. May the power of our Lord Jesus Christ keep me faithful to himself! And now, my dearest friend, how my heart yearns for you! How I long to see you come to this Saviour and be at peace! What can I say? I feel that words are useless. I can only pray for you; and this, God granting me the ability, I will do until you are brought into this sheltered fold, of which Christ is the compassionate Shepherd. I do not feel as if I could *argue* the subject with you; for though "I know that my Redeemer liveth," I know also that it is not by *argument*, but from *conviction*, that you will embrace the truth; and this NO words can adequately express. My heart is too full to write more at present; yet this one thing I may say—that no motive for work was ever half so powerful as the thought that I am now working for my dear Saviour. It seems to me that, through Christ strengthening me, I can do all things.'

"To another friend she says, 'On the 13th of March, I went to the prayer-meeting at Jayne's Hall out of mere curiosity. I took my seat in the crowded room with a feeling of infinite superiority to the benighted souls around me who could find any comfort in such scenes of fanatical excitement. But, irresistibly, a different feeling stole over me. I realized that the Spirit of God was present there in a way never witnessed by me before. My own poor, philosophical religion seemed vain and dead in view of the whole-souled earnestness which I saw and felt around me. Here was something above and beyond my experience; and, though I had gone in to criticize and scoff, I sat there in tears, with a bitter sense of the insufficiency of *all* my philosophy. For the first time, my faith in my preconceived opinion was shaken. These worshippers *knew* whom they believed: I did not, and I could not be at peace.'"

PERSONAL EFFORT

To a careful observer of the work of God in this city during the last year, there are two things in reference to which there will be little or no dispute. The first is the UNION of Christians in their spirit. "We are all one man's sons"—the sons of ISRAEL. The second is the INDIVIDUALITY of Christians in all the various fields of Christian exertion. "Lord, what wilt thou have ME to do?" The question of service is asked directly of the Lord, the commission received from him, and not at second-hand from someone else. *My* presence is wanted: am I there? *My* prayers are called for: are they forthcoming? There are souls to be saved, and I must do *my* part towards saving them: who are they, and where are they to be found?

PERSONAL OBLIGATION TO BRING SINNERS TO REPENTANCE

We think it safe to say, this has recently been felt in this city to an extent that has never been known in it before. Doing good merely by donation, or deputy, or proxy, has failed to satisfy the conscience. Each man has his own burden and his own cross, or he is not at work as he should be.

The extent to which some of our young men particularly have been blessed in their labours has been remarkable indeed. Six, eight, ten, and even more of their companions won to Christ through their immediate instrumentality—such is the history of not a few who thus sincerely and earnestly devoted themselves to the work of the Lord. By conversing with a friend, by inviting him to church or prayer-meeting, by introducing him to a Christian minister, by giving him a book or tract—above all, by making him the special subject of prayer in secret—simple as these means appear, they have been all-powerful, through the blessing of God, to produce the desired result.

HOLY JOY

"Never was I so happy in all my life," said a young convert, after taking up the cross for Christ at a prayer-meeting. "I always knew what Jesus had done for me, but this was the first time *I ever really felt that I had done anything for Jesus.* My joy at conversion was as nothing compared with that which I now feel on entering into *service!*"

A Mission Prayer-Meeting

In a short but thickly-populated street in the upper part of the city, two young men were seen one afternoon endeavouring to find some room in which to hold a prayer-meeting. Having passed from one end of the street to the other without finding any house for this purpose, the wife of a good-natured skeptic suggested a wish to have such a meeting in their house. Laughingly assenting to the proposition, the meeting was accordingly appointed. For four or five weeks it was continued without any apparent fruit; but, though the blessing "tarried," it came in the end. First the wife was converted; then a number of others—the *twenty-seventh* being the husband. Afterwards, it became necessary to have two meetings instead of one, and some forty conversions, it is hoped, may be traced to that little meeting. What is to prevent the establishment of hundreds of similar meetings all over the city? And why not expect from them similar results?

The Runner's Bible-Class

During the latter part of the winter, a series of meetings, which lasted some seven weeks without intermission, were held for the special benefit of that class of boys known as the "runners" with the engines. During the progress of the meeting, several professed to have experienced a change of heart; and their subsequent conduct has given good evidence of the truth of their profession. On the termination of the prayer-meetings, a Bible-class was organized—to be held once a week—for the instruction of the young converts and for any others who might wish to attend. The movement unexpectedly proved to be a very popular one. That a class of young men, whose ages range from eighteen to twenty, the regular *habitués* of the corner, those who were supposed to be almost beyond hope, should meet regularly on a week-day evening for the purpose of receiving instruction from the word of God, and of engaging afterwards in prayer with and for one another, a year ago would have seemed almost impossible. But our readers may rest assured that the fact is even as we declare it.

A similar movement has been in progress among the "newsboys," showing that they, too, are accessible—as also among various other classes of neglected youth. The additions to the Sabbath-schools during the last year have been very large. Seventy-four schools (being less than one-third of the whole number) have reported *fifteen hundred and forty-six* conversions during the year. Various other movements are now in progress among the youth—even more interesting, some of them, than any we have stated; but they are so recent in their origin that, for the present, it is better to refer to them merely in the general. When, however, the proper time does come to mention them, it will be to many equally the occasion of surprise and joy.

THE MEETING WHERE GOD WAS

At the commencement of this revival, some fifteen young men, members of respectable and well-known families in Philadelphia, were banded together as a sort of club. Like hundreds, and perhaps thousands of similar circles in the city, they were in the habit of meeting every afternoon and evening in various drinking-saloons, and sometimes in their own homes, to play cards, to drink wine, and spend their nights in revelry. Thus were they all in the broad road to ruin, when it pleased God to arrest one of their number by his Spirit and lead him to a place of worship. Little did he think, on returning home at two o'clock the night before, that the next afternoon he would be in the house of God. But the same mighty leaven was beginning to work in his heart that had already found its way into the hearts of so many others. Lingering at the close of the service and attracting the notice of the minister by his ill-concealed agitation, a conversation ensued between them as to the worth of the soul and how far he himself was interested in this matter personally. All his impressions thus greatly deepened, he determined to abandon the club and throw himself in the way of other and better influences. The following week, he met with one of his old companions with whom he had been the most intimate, who rallied him on the change that had come over him and proposed a visit to the circus. Admitting the reality of the change, he endeavoured to persuade his companion that his new life was a better one for him than his old one, and induce him to adopt a similar one for himself. Once and again they passed the door of the circus during their walk; but, their conversation becoming more and more absorbing, the friend, now also awakened, returned with him to his house. It was not long before both friends were rejoicing in Him who loves to be called the "Friend of sinners."

The conversion of these two young men was not without its effect on the rest of their companions; and, for a time, the operations of the club were completely suspended. Hearing, after some weeks that it was about to be revived, it was agreed between the two to anticipate the movement by a prayer-meeting. Such a meeting was accordingly appointed at the house of one of the converts, to which he invited not only all his old associates of the club, but some of his new-found friends in the Christian Association. The scene was certainly a most extraordinary one. Those who, in that same house, had gathered around the card-table, to drink the intoxicating cup, to sing the bacchanalian song, and indulge freely in the language of profanity, now met to worship God in praise and prayer! From this time forward nothing more was heard of reviving the club. The prayer-meeting took its place: the Bible was substituted for the decanter, and the hymn-book for the pack of cards. Each successive meeting seemed to increase in interest; until, at length, in the early part of the summer, one meeting in particular was held, which will be long remembered by those who were present as "the meeting where God was." The room was closely filled with about fifty young men; and it was evident, from the very commencement of the meeting, that God was in the midst of them. As soon as the meeting was thrown open, one young man arose and asked them to pray for him, as he had just determined, by the help of God, to be a Christian. First one prayer was offered for him, and then another, all remaining on their knees, and pleading fervently with God, not only for this friend but for every other there that was seeking Jesus.

At the close of this prayer, a third commenced praying. He prayed that God would lead the Christians then present to pray for him. He prayed in the broken accents of a foreigner—as one "who had no friend;" who had "left a dear mother far over the waves;" who was a stranger in a strange land; and who wanted "to have Jesus to be *his* friend," who was the "friend and Saviour of his mother in Europe." Tears were seen streaming from every eye; and a fourth brother took up the burden and prayed, while they were still kneeling, for him who had last prayed, as "no longer a stranger, but a brother!" The company then all arose from their knees weeping, and for some time not a man could summon the courage, or collect himself sufficiently, to say a single word. The leader, in a subdued and almost inaudible voice, gave out the hymn,

"Alas! and did my Saviour bleed?"

and sweetly did the melting hearts of the singers flow out in the channel of its harmonies! The hymn over, fervent and affectionate were the appeals that came from the lips of those who tried to address the meeting; and soon another rose, saying, "Pray for me, brothers. I, too, will be for Christ." Another arose with a similar request. At the close of the meeting, three more announced their resolution to come out on the Lord's side. The next afternoon, at the "Diligent" prayer-meeting, another young man rose and said that at the meeting in Spruce Street last evening he too had found the Saviour. The blessedness of that evening will never be effaced from the memories of those who enjoyed the precious privilege of being there, "where God was." Eight young men coming out from the world comprised nearly every unconverted man in the room; and the conversation with the rejoicing penitents after the meeting was over was, if anything, even more delightful than the meeting itself.

From that night the meeting was made a permanent one. From week to week the hymn-books, camp-stools, etc. are carried round to the parlours of different private residences. Up to December 1st, twenty-three meetings had been held, always largely attended, some of them numbering over a hundred young men; and, from a careful estimate, there is every reason to believe that through their instrumentality at least twenty souls have been "born again," and led to rejoice in God their Saviour! Why should not every town and village see a similar prayer-meeting? And why should not many more such clubs in our city experience a similar transformation? Who doubts that it would be better for the young men themselves, for their parents, for their wives and children, and for the real welfare of the entire community?

One witness more, and we close the record. As if to leave no possible doubt on any candid mind as to the fact that this was the work of God, and not of man, it has pleased God to send his Holy Spirit into the *solitary cells of the prison*. The letter of the "Moral Instructor" needs no comment. The theory of "sympathy," to whatever extent it may apply elsewhere, has certainly nothing to recommend it here.

PHILADELPHIA, Oct. 30, 1858.

DEAR SIR:—Agreeably to your request, I send to you the following brief statement of the religious influence which has for some months past pervaded the Eastern Penitentiary.

"I may premise that during the past three years there has been very little, if any, genuine feeling regarding the interests of the soul and eternity, I have endeavoured to present the truths of the gospel to the minds of the prisoners, but with a desponding spirit, having little hope that any would be led to seek deliverance from the wrath to come. During the early part of the remarkable movement which has awakened public attention in our own and other cities, and over all our land I was led from prudential considerations to withhold from the inmates, in my Sabbath ministrations, any statement of what was transpiring without, lest the mere influence of human sympathies should awaken a corresponding excitement within the prison, which might pass away like the early cloud or the morning dew.

"Some time towards the latter end of March last, the prisoner who aided me in the distribution of the books which are issued weekly from the library, called my attention to a fact which had arrested his attention; that there was an unusual demand for religious books, a kind rarely called for previously. This was not immediately attended to, owing to the exhausting and hurried labours of that day. But subsequently he directed my attention to this matter more impressively, adding, 'Had you not better attend to it?' I replied, 'Yes: let me know who they are who take such books.' I was somewhat aroused by the interest with which *he* regarded this apparent concern on the part of other prisoners, suspecting that he too was not wholly indifferent to the momentous question, 'What must I do to be saved?' I conversed with him seriously in relation to it, and urged him to a careful examination of the fifty-third chapter of the Prophecy of Isaiah. Soon after this, a deep anxiety was manifested by him, (it may be proper to state that the individual here referred to was a very intelligent Jew, whose term of service had nearly expired) which I trust has resulted in his conversion. I have never known an instance of professed conversion more satisfactory.

"On one occasion, attending a prayer-meeting at Jayne's Hall, prayer was requested in behalf of a young man recently consigned to the Eastern Penitentiary, of whom it was announced soon after that prayer had been answered, and that he was converted. These events, occurring without any direct efforts of an exciting kind within the prison, induced the adoption of means to ascertain to what extent this influence prevailed. On the following Sabbath, after the sermon, I expressed a hope that the Spirit of God was operating on the hearts of some of the inmates, and requested that as many as wished to have personal conversation on the subject of religion would signify it by quietly dropping a piece of paper, containing their designating number, outside of the doors of their cells.

"This was responded to by twelve or thirteen in the corridor where I then preached. The same plan was adopted by visiting brethren who preached on successive Sabbaths in other parts of the house, until the number who were desirous of religious converse and prayer exceeded fifty persons. In a short time some ten or twelve professed to have found peace in believing on the Lord Jesus Christ. Others continue to exhibit evidences of sincere desire for salvation, while some have apparently relapsed into a state of indifference. Some five or six who gave evidence of a saving change, having served out their time in prison, have been discharged—all of them, I believe, having continued to act consistently with their professions up to that period. One young man died not long since, expressing a steadfast hope of salvation through the atoning merits of Jesus. The present aspect of the prison is less interesting: few, if any, new instances of conviction have been noticed. Owing to the pressure of multiplied duties, my opportunities of becoming acquainted with such cases are quite limited.

"In visiting and inquiring among those who were the subjects of this awakening, I was struck with the singular coincidence of their attention being called to the subject of religion at about the same time; two or three in the month of January, and nearly all the rest in and through the month of February, at which time there was repeated and earnest prayer offered for prisoners at the meeting in Jayne's Hall.

"That this Divine influence visiting this prison at that period was in answer to those prayers, I cannot doubt; and would greatly rejoice if, in the noonday and other prayer-meetings, the prisoners could share in the fervent, effectual offerings presented at the throne of grace. Will you please make this request on our behalf, and oblige.

Yours affectionately,

T. L., Moral Instructor

In view of these, and a multitude of similar facts, of which these stand only as the imperfect representatives, we feel bound in all honour and conscience, both as men and as Christians, to express to our city, our common-wealth, our country, and the world at large, our most solemn and undoubting belief that this last year in the religious history of Philadelphia has been "a year of the right hand of the Most High," and that many of its days have been days of Pentecost indeed. The great question is, "WHAT HATH GOD WROUGHT?" and not, "What has been done by man?" Almost as by a voice from the Excellent Glory, we seem to hear the emphatic declaration, "Not by might, nor by power, but by my Spirit, saith the Lord of hosts." "They shall come, and shall declare his righteousness unto a people that shall be born, that HE HATH DONE THIS." *The human instrumentality in this matter is as nothing compared with the Divine agency.*

Individual Christians, lay or clerical; individual churches, whether belonging to this denomination or the other; denominations themselves, whether larger or smaller, all as with one accord, with no anxiety to challenge relative superiority, no jealousy to adjust rival or peculiar claims, humble, grateful, and rejoicing, meet here as in the great congregation, in the one glorious ascription of praise: "Not unto us, O Lord, not unto us, but unto thy name give glory, for thy mercy and for thy truth's sake." As it was *"the pouring forth anew of that life which Christ brought into the world"* that will alone account for the Reformation, so a new installment of the Divine life is the only theory on which we can satisfactorily account for this "Great Awakening." We assume that it is of God until there are those who are bold enough, and subtle enough, to prove it otherwise. Occasional indiscretions on the part of any who have been the subjects of His work, or the humble agents in carrying it forward, have as little to do with the real character of the work as the bubble on the surface has to do in determining the character of the stream. In the wise and carefully-chosen language of another, "Let us carefully distinguish between what we are to set down to the dishonour of man, and what we are to be thankful for to the praise of God. As, in a single instance of the power of his converting grace, we are not the less persuaded of the genuineness of the work because the old nature, though subdued, still appears, so let us judge of a more general work!" Thus far, as compared with the purest revivals of the past, the absence of extravagance of any kind is extraordinary to a perfect marvel. Never in their social devotions were the people of God in the enjoyment of wider or more unrestricted liberty, and never was this liberty less perverted. "During the last week," (the last week in June) said a brother, "I have attended no less than five-and-twenty different prayer-meetings.

Going there calmly and deliberately, for the express purpose of carefully observing their spiritual character and of studying out as far as possible the philosophy of such unwonted gatherings of the people of God, looking at them in every possible light of which I am capable, the candid and unavoidable conclusion to which I have come is this:—THEY ARE OF GOD!" The testimony of the great Anniversary Meeting at Jayne's Hall, Nov. 3, 1858, was cordially and unanimously the same:—"THIS IS THE LORD'S DOING: IT IS MARVELLOUS IN OUR EYES!"

The many and various LESSONS from these facts, as to the nature of prayer; the duty of intercession; the NOON PRAYER-MEETING, the expediency not only of a Sabbath day in every week, but of a Sabbath hour in every day; the value of CHRISTIAN UNION; the importance of personal, individual effort for the conversion of souls; the newly-opened field of "UNION MISSIONS," in which it has not only been demonstrated that Christians *can* pray and work together, *but that it is for their own mutual benefit and the advantage of the common cause thus to do;* the true principles of reformation and of CITY EVANGELIZATION; the development of latent power in the church; the guilt of those who have opposed this work, or who have been indifferent to it, or who have been mere absorbents of it by a luxurious spiritual sympathy, giving neither of their means nor energies to carry it forward—these are fruitful and suggestive topics, that we leave to each of our readers to carry out at their leisure. God hath indeed "done great things for us, whereof we are glad;" but whether, after having thus been brought within sight of the promised land, and been made to taste of the rich clusters of Eshcol, we shall go up at once and possess the land, or whether we shall turn back again into the wilderness, leaving it to another and better generation to complete the conquest which has been so auspiciously commenced, "the day will declare it."

Prayerless, Christless soul, whether in the church or out of it— you who have thus far lived through this revival like an "island of ice in a sea of fire,"—who have been like "the heat in the desert, that knoweth not when good cometh,"—especially are these pages designed for you. "We cannot but speak the things which we have seen and heard;" and as though our souls were in your souls' stead are we anxious that you should receive our testimony. "TO-DAY," the Holy Ghost saith, "if ye will hear his voice, harden not your hearts." Not to hear that voice *is* to harden your hearts. As in the time of Whitefield, in many places where he preached, those who remained unconverted until the close of that great revival remained so until their death, so may it be with you. Since the commencement of this work, warnings have multiplied around us on every hand. Are you an unbeliever in the gospel? We could tell you of three friends, who, around their cups, agreed that the first of them to die should give the others the benefit of his experience. Very soon the opportunity was afforded. The testimony was given, and as the affrighted friend carried the news to his companion, his first exclamation was, *"We had better believe it all!* Neither you nor I would want to die as he is dying!" Are you a Sabbath-breaker? We can tell of one who broke away with curses from his father and mother on the morning of a Sabbath day to go sailing, and by the time the sun was down was brought home a corpse. Are you postponing the claims of the gospel to a more convenient season? So was one who was hurried off by a violent and unexpected disease: no time on that death-bed for any preparation. Have you even fixed the period when you will come to the Lord Jesus Christ, and believe in him to the saving of your soul? So did another young man. "My next birthday will soon come round, and then I will give my heart to Christ." These were his words on a Sabbath morning as he was leaving the church after a very solemn sermon. On Tuesday, while exhibiting his strength in lifting a heavy box, he burst a blood-vessel, proving almost immediately fatal. His birthday came, but where was he? Are you resisting the Holy Spirit, refusing to yield at once to those convictions of guilt and danger that would bring you to the foot of the Cross for pardon and eternal life? It may be with you as with another, who hesitated too long before resolving to be on the Lord's side. About to enter Jayne's Hall, and meeting an ungodly companion, he allowed himself to be drawn another way. An infidel book was placed in his hand: he read it, and all at once it became as dark within as the smoke of the pit could make it! In a single moment he was given over to blindness of mind and hardness of heart. Belief in God's word, conviction of sin, every purpose of good, all vanished; he was made to know by a fearful experience that to quench the Holy Spirit was to leave the soul in utter and, for aught that appears to the contrary thus far, in eternal darkness. Wait not for deeper convictions. The question is, "Are you *really* convinced?" not, "How *deeply* are you convinced of sin?"

" 'THE DOOR WAS SHUT:' that was the text," said a young convert, "that went to my heart, and awakened me as to my danger." "Isaiah 12," said another: "that was the chapter that brought me consolation." "My verse," said another, "was John 6:37:—'Him that cometh to me, I will in NO WISE cast out.' "

May God, in infinite mercy, grant to every reader of this tract that he too may learn the great lesson that MAN is a SINNER, that CHRIST is a SAVIOUR, and ACT ACCORDINGLY!

SUPPLEMENT

The Contrast

To look back to the state of religion in Philadelphia two years ago is to be reminded of Israel in the land of Egypt or of Babylon, in the days of Nehemiah, Isaiah, Ezekiel, Joel, and Jeremiah. We almost shudder to think how far, how very far, the flock had wandered from the fold, and to what a sad extent "the rivers of water were dried up, and the fire had consumed the pastures of the wilderness."

But, "blessed be the name of the Lord our God, who hath dealt wondrously with us," "the years that the locust hath eaten, the canker-worm, and the caterpillar, and the palmer-worm, he hath restored." From the beginning to the end of this ever-memorable year of the Lord, to those who have been fully engaged in the work it has been but one continued "feast of harvest." Each season has witnessed to the power of God, each month to his faithfulness, each week to his mercy, and each day to his love. All its days have been as "the days of heaven upon earth." We have seen no reason whatever, even for a single moment, to doubt the truth of our position—that this is indeed "the finger of God." Like the streams from the mountains of California, that leave behind their rich deposits of gold, or like the overflowing of the Nile, that leaves its fertilizing sediment on every inch of soil over which it passes, so has it been with these "streams from Lebanon," —this "river of God," which is "so full of water." With one accord, we believe it will be universally admitted that such a year as the past this city has never seen before.

"The ploughman overtakes the reaper," the "threshing reaches unto the vintage," and "the treading of grapes to the time of sowing." Once more has the precious promise been fulfilled, "He shall cause them that come of Jacob to take root; Israel shall blossom and bud, and fill the face of the world with fruit." (Isa. 27:6) Because of its marvelous abundance, we complete the circle of the year with thanksgiving and with holy joy.

Perhaps there is nothing that will better show the vitality of the Union Prayer-Meetings, and the steady interest manifested in them, than the manner in which their anniversaries have been observed.

THE DAILY MORNING PRAYER-MEETING,
(Buttonwood Street, Above Fifth. Service At 8 A.M.)

The anniversary of this meeting was held on Wednesday, the 16th of March. From the very beginning, there has been an earnest, tender spirit about this meeting that makes it the true successor of the "Bochim" elsewhere described in these pages. If anywhere inquiring souls are sure of sympathy, it is here; and from week to week, almost constantly, have there been those who have availed themselves of it.

THE BETHEL MEETING,
(Front Street, below Chestnut. Service at noon.)

This Union Prayer-Meeting observed its anniversary Tuesday, the 22d of March; and a very sweet and precious season it was. As the name indicates, there is special interest taken by this meeting of sailors. During the year, many of them have been present to stir up the zeal of their brethren by such exhortations as none but sailors can give. "When I was far off upon the sea," "in my bunk," or "aloft," "on the look-out," or "at the wheel," "the Lord met me, and convinced me of my sin; and I am here to-day to say, PRAY ON, brethren; PRAY ON. Your prayers are being answered!" How often have we heard such declarations as these, and always with new and peculiar interest!

The remarkable feature in this meeting, however, is the fervour and freedom of its CHRISTIAN FELLOWSHIP. "Why," said a brother, "I can compare them to nothing else than a little band of disciples who are in love with Christ, and have fallen in love with each other for his sake." From this point as a centre the holy leaven of brotherly love has quietly and almost imperceptibly diffused itself into many other meetings. Whoever went into that heavenly atmosphere was sure to take some of it away with him. Ask any who attend this meeting how it came to receive such a character, and all the explanation they can give is this: —"All that is peculiar in our meeting we trace to the fact that, from the very commencement of it, we determined to put honour on the word of God—not to use it merely as a motto and read a few verses as a matter of form, but to READ A GOOD, HONEST CHAPTER, and, asking the Holy Spirit, the only Teacher of the word, to 'engraft' it in our hearts, make that the staple of our prayers and exhortations." Thus it is that they know what it is to have fellowship with the Father in love, with the Son in grace, with the Holy Spirit in consolation, and, consequently, understand the fellowship of the saints to an extent we have very seldom seen elsewhere. It is indeed a "Bethel;" and why should there not be a similar meeting in every village throughout the land?

NOON PRAYER-MEETING, (Formerly at Jayne's Hall; now usually held in Sansom Street Church.)

To-day, March 26, the attendance was as large, the "requests" as numerous, the prayers as earnest, the exhortations as pungent, and every link in the golden chain of Christian union as bright and perfect, as ever. Only where the Comforter is *absent* is there coldness and division; and, thanks unspeakable to Him who is our Advocate above, the Holy Dove is with us still. Even within a few days past, some of the most marked and wonderful answers to prayer have been witnessed by us of any we have yet seen.

"LOVEST THOU ME?"

A few weeks ago, the twenty-first chapter of John was read and briefly commented upon by the pastor who led the meeting. It pleased God to make the question of Christ strike home to the heart of many a Peter with unwonted power. The chapter was read at the other union meetings, and made the theme of exhortations; lectures, and even of sermons; and incident after incident might be given to show with what power it became to many "the present truth," the "word in season." The following Thursday, a lady was seen at the close of the services with her head bowed, and so totally absorbed in thought as to be entirely unconscious that the receding tide of worshippers had left her alone in the very midst of the church. "Is it for yourself or someone else that your heart is so burdened?" inquired a friend. "It is for myself. I feel as if I *must* be able to answer that question, 'LOVEST THOU ME?' *or I shall die!*" The tearless agony with which these words were uttered we do not pretend to describe. Many were the prayers that were offered on her behalf; and it was not long before she also could say, "Lord, thou knowest all things: thou knowest that *I* love thee!" Thus has God often honoured his word; and occasionally a single text has filled a whole meeting.

EXPERIENCE OF YOUNG CONVERTS

Take that of one or two of them, just as it has fallen into our hands.

"The first thing I felt after standing up for prayer was that I must now 'Stand up for Jesus' and labour for the souls of others. At once I found myself talking in a manner totally different from anything I had ever uttered before, and I began to listen to myself in perfect astonishment. It was as though some other person was using my lips and speaking through them. It seemed to me now so perfectly natural to love God that I could not help it; and I felt that I loved every man, woman, and child in the world. When I prayed, the expression *my* Father and *my* God fell spontaneously from my lips with a depth of meaning that was full of comfort to me. The following Sabbath, the services of the house of God were unspeakably precious to me. My great and burning desire then was to bring others to the Saviour, whose love so filled my own heart. I felt as though I could convert half the world could I but get an opportunity to talk to them. Next to the happiness of the knowledge of pardoned sin would be that of a soul converted to God in answer to my prayers. This also was granted to me.... I have lived a lifetime in this glorious year which is now drawing to a close. Religion becomes simpler to me every day, and I find it all summed up in this single sentence: 'Looking unto Jesus!' "

TESTIMONY OF ONE OF OUR OLDEST PASTORS

"One hundred and two converts have been added to us this last year; and I can truly say that, in all the revivals through which I have passed, I have never known one in which the converts have pleased me so well as those in this present gracious visitation. Two associations—one male and the other female, most of them these converts—now sustain between them as many as *thirty* prayer-meetings, many of them at private houses—from which they bring to me many inquiring souls."

DILIGENT PRAYER-MEETING

This has now become the regular EVENING daily prayer-meeting, and all that we have said of the noon meeting is equally true of it. The number of conversions has recently been greater here than in any other meeting. Fifteen minutes before the close of the services, the opportunity is invariably given to any persons who desire the prayers of the meeting to rise; and scores of instances could be given in which, when asking and receiving the prayers of others on their behalf, *God has heard their own.*

On the 25th of March, one of the firemen of this company rose and said, "I feel it a duty pressing upon me to acknowledge that this is my birthday—my first spiritual anniversary. This day, one year ago, I gave my heart to God! The year, how short! and yet long enough for me to find the reality and happiness in the religion of Jesus Christ. Suddenly, without a moment's warning, I have found myself in the midst of danger and my life in peril; but God has watched over and protected me. I have not lived up to my privileges as I should have done; but my experience is this—that the nearer I live to God the nearer I want to live; the more I labour for him, the more I want to labour! Happy thought! Each year I now live I am one year nearer my home! One word to those who are still out of Christ. Each time you have mercy offered to you and you reject it, the harder your heart becomes, until no impression is made upon it whatever. Bear in mind the solemn words of God, 'My Spirit shall not always strive,' and accept pardon while you have time and opportunity."

QUAKERTOWN

We have very recent and gratifying intelligence from our dear brethren in this place. "Persuasion Hut," as their edifice is sometimes called by its opposers, is still doing its good work, and "The Tabernacles," as its worshippers are termed by way of reproach, give good evidence that they are indeed "the temples of the Holy Ghost." The work is extending into the regions beyond.

THE FRIENDS' PRAYER-MEETING

Two pious ladies, with their relatives, long intimate associates of Joseph John Gurney and Elizabeth Fry, living in a rural district near the city, which was destitute of all the ordinary means of grace, and feeling in their own hearts the influence of the mighty wave of spiritual awakening sweeping over the land, united with some young men of the Christian Association in sustaining in a schoolhouse in the neighbourhood a union prayer-meeting. As the meetings continued, the interest deepened; and in the stormiest weather, when the roads and lanes leading to the place of meeting seemed almost impassable, the room would be crowded to excess. At length the cloud, big with mercy, broke upon and baptized the waiting assembly. After an unusually long and interesting meeting, while the brethren were singing some of the songs of Zion, as if still unwilling to separate, the attention of a brother was directed to a young man bowing his head upon a form, who seemed to invite the attention of someone who cared for his soul. Scarcely had the brother reached him and laid his hand upon his shoulder, and said, "My brother," when the young man leaned his head upon the brother's breast and burst into such a convulsive flood of tears as well-nigh unmanned all present. While thus refusing to be comforted, a young lady came up, and, putting her arms around his neck, joined her tears with his, and together they wept to such a degree that the brethren could not refrain from weeping with them. At length they began to tell of Jesus, who himself wept for dying men. Till nearly midnight the cries for mercy went up from this group, echoed back by others in another part of the room, also broken-hearted on account of their sin, and the brethren gladly continued to hold up the cross and point to Him who taketh away the sins of the world. It subsequently appeared that the lady was a bride, and the gentleman her husband, to whom she had been united but four days before. By the next meeting both of them were rejoicing in Christ; and the week following, another husband and wife, with several others, were soon following in their footsteps. The meeting is still continued with unabated interest.

THE MEETING WHERE GOD WAS

...still continues as a meeting where God is. A pastor at whose house it was recently held, among other things, writes as follows:—"Very memorable was it because of the exalted Christian fellowship that was enjoyed at it. It was a season of rejoicing—of happy exultation. Everyone felt that Jesus was there talking with his chosen on the way, and, oh, how their hearts burned within them! The prevailing spirit of the meeting was that of thankful rejoicing in the fullness of the great salvation. 'Jesus and Jesus only was the essence of every song, the end of every exhortation, and the burden of every prayer. Heart flowed into heart in the gushing sympathy of love to Christ and joy in him; while all felt that they were upon the Mount, and that God was giving them precious glimpses of his glory as he revealed the infinite fullness of his grace in Jesus. That little company had many cares to trouble them and many sins to make them weary, but oh, what a blessed retreat they found on that memorable night, as they shut out the world and gathered, as the friends of the Crucified, around the mercy-seat, and hid themselves in the cleft of the rock while the glory of the Lord passed by. The joy of the Lord was filling their souls, and as hand was clasped in hand as they sung their parting song, and every face beamed with the radiance of the pure joy which the Master had given, how rich and full was the experience of those who once walked in the ways of sinful pleasure, that the greatest happiness which can be found on earth is that which springs up in the hearts of those who are thus made by the grace of God 'to sit together in heavenly places in Christ Jesus!' Many were they who tasted of the grapes of Eshcol on that precious evening."

The Tract "Pentecost" an Answer to Prayer

Shortly after his conversion, a young convert commenced a "Religious Album," in which to record incidents illustrating the mighty power of the prayer of faith, and the simple means employed by God to produce the most stupendous results. The first sentence in this book read as follows:— "I dedicate this book to Almighty God by prayer, and with the fervent wish, hope, and belief that he may bless what is herein contained to many of God's saints, in strengthening their faith, and be the means, under God, of leading some soul into a saving knowledge of the truth." The dedication concludes with this remarkable expression:—"Now, little volume, go forth on thy mission of love and mercy; and may eternity reveal the results of thy mission here on earth!"

It was this album that first suggested the idea of "Pentecost" and supplied some of its most valuable pages. The tract and the album are identical. The "little volume" has indeed "gone forth." Ten thousand copies already in circulation—republished beyond the ocean, with an introduction of twenty pages by Professor Gibson, of Belfast—and now the second edition, with the Supplement, stereotyped: if such is the beginning of its history, what will be the end? If, as we have now the evidence before us, some who have read it in private, or heard it read in various prayer-meetings have been converted through its instrumentality, is it too much to ask the prayer of the Christian reader, who now lays it down, that it may be blessed to the conversion of many more? Dear reader still out of Christ, will you not pray that its perusal may lead you also to say,

"I the chief of sinners am:
But Jesus died for me"?

PHILADELPHIA, March 26, 1859.
THE END.

Stereotyped by L. Johnson & Co.
PHILADELPHIA